BUILT FOR LEARNING

A UNIFIED ARCHITECTURAL VISION FOR
THE UNIVERSITY OF DENVER

"Make no little plans;
they have no magic to stir men's blood ..."

— Daniel Burnham

CONTENTS

INTRODUCTION

By Chancellor Robert D. Coombe

In the latter years of the 1990s, much was written about the technological tidal wave passing through higher education. One read that Internet-based distance education was the future and that bricks and mortar campuses were dinosaurs that simply would not compete in the brave new world just ahead. Instead, it was said, higher education of the not-so-distant future would occur in a cyber-environment where classes were online, anytime and anywhere, where students would connect with one another in chat rooms, and where text messages would be the carrier of faculty-student interaction. Technology would sound the death knell of traditional campuses.

Of course, such predictions have not been borne out. Technology has certainly expanded the reach of higher education and enriched the teaching and learning environment, but campuses are still special places that provide an optimum environment for learning and creativity. It is still true that thinking, learning, reflection, and the generation of new ideas are deeply human activities that can be stimulated and vastly enhanced by place and context.

Those of us who love universities take pleasure in the fact that these special places loom large in the public's imagination. I frequently hear people talk about how they especially enjoy college towns and university neighborhoods. Some of this fondness can be traced to campus activities like the sporting events, plays, concerts, film screenings, and lectures that most of us associate with university life. But university campuses are about much more than entertainment. They capture the affection of the public because the notions of personal growth, learning, and idea generation are so particularly human. They touch the deepest recesses of our hearts and minds. They represent the highest aspiration of a people and a culture. For so many of us, the university campus symbolizes unbounded possibility.

As one walks across the University of Denver campus, it's hard to suppress that sense of possibility, of the open door to the future. When I stroll our red-brick pathways, I round a bend to see a tower reaching for the sky. I see a distant peak promising the frontier. I see, in the stately trees and solid structures around me, a place that has played an essential role in the evolution of our city, state, and region. We have made history here, and we continue to do so every day. Perhaps most of all, I see a place where countless lives have taken shape, where countless ideas have been born, for generations.

From the Ritchie Center to the Newman Center, from Nelson Hall to F.W. Olin Hall, our new buildings acknowledge our past and reflect our long history in this particular place. The standards that define these buildings, the standards set by former Chancellor Dan Ritchie and architect Cab Childress — quality construction, materials with integrity, design that accommodates changing realities — have set the bar for all our projects. These standards are on display in Nagel Hall, our new residence hall completed in fall 2008, and they shape the plans for all our future projects, like Katherine A. Ruffatto Hall, the new home for the Morgridge College of Education.

At some universities, reverence for tradition has been taken too far, stifling the appetite for change. The ivy-clad buildings, walls, and enclosed quads stand silent, as if to say "whoa there, not so fast." These campuses create that time-worn image of the ivory tower that is somehow defending itself from the chaos and uncertainty of "real" life. At the University of Denver, ours is a culture that delights in change and embraces it as opportunity. People are our business, and we hope to graduate students whose lives will change the world for the better. Ideas are our business, and the purpose of ideas is change. So, change is our business as well, and that philosophy is reflected in the culture of our community and in the buildings, spaces, and rhythm of our campus.

The University of Denver campus delights the eye and cultivates our lasting affection. What I love best about it, though, is that it positions the university, the city, and our region for a future we can only begin to imagine.

PROJECTS CURRENTLY IN PROGRESS INCLUDE KATHERINE A. RUFFATTO HALL, TOP, HOME TO THE MORGRIDGE COLLEGE OF EDUCATION. A RENOVATION WILL TRANSFORM THE EXTERIOR OF THE LIBRARY AND BRING THE INTERIOR INTO THE TWENTY-FIRST CENTURY. THE SITE PLAN FOR THE SCHOOL OF ENGINEERING AND COMPUTER SCIENCE, BOTTOM, POSITIONS THE FACILITY ON THE SOUTH SIDE OF CAMPUS NEAR F.W. OLIN HALL.

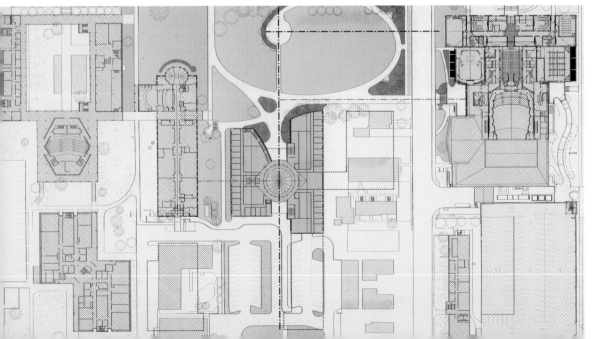

"The founders and promoters of this University believe not only in power but in beauty and grace. ... It shall be thronged by the lovers and seekers of the beautiful for centuries to come.

... As Athens was the eye of Greece, so may Denver be the place toward which the pilgrim feet of Americans seeking health, refinement, and education, shall gladly come."

— BISHOP HENRY WHITE WARREN
  On the occasion of the laying of the University Hall cornerstone, April 3, 1890

PEOPLE CAME FROM FAR AND WIDE TO WITNESS THE LAYING OF THE UNIVERSITY HALL CORNERSTONE. FOR COLORADANS IN THE 1890s, A CONSTRUCTION PROJECT OF THIS MAGNITUDE WAS BOTH A CURIOSITY AND A SYMBOL OF PROMISING DAYS AHEAD.

When ground was broken on University Hall — the first building on the University of Denver's University Park campus — the institution had already weathered twenty-six years of tumult. Its first quarter century was marked by financial uncertainty, by the same booms and busts that characterized the Centennial State's economic life. For school officials and supporters on hand for the 1890 groundbreaking, the construction of University Hall represented a new beginning — an attempt to lay the cornerstone for a new Athens.

UNIVERSITY HALL

Over the next century, the University Park campus added buildings, gardens, and greens, all constructed in response to pressing needs and all designed in accordance with the architectural vision favored at the time. By the 1990s, it was clear that some of these efforts had withstood the test of time, while others had outlived their usefulness. It was also clear that, to meet the challenges of the coming century, the university would need to add a host of buildings and update many others. It would need to create a unified campus with learning spaces to stimulate thinking, foster creativity, build community, and nurture memories. Its leaders would need to re-imagine Athens.

To begin that task, they first looked to the past.

TWO YEARS AFTER MOVING TO THE COLORADO TERRITORY, JOHN EVANS, TOP, LAUNCHED THE COLORADO SEMINARY. ITS FIRST HOME WAS IN A STURDY BUILDING IN DOWNTOWN DENVER. ITS ARCHITECTURE REFERENCED STYLES AND TRADITIONS FROM THE MIDWEST AND NEW ENGLAND. THE BUILDING'S ARCHED WINDOWS COMMUNICATED AN AIR OF DIGNITY AND SUGGESTED THAT THE BUILDING WAS DEDICATED TO LOFTY PURSUITS.

A BUILDING SET IN STONE

The University of Denver began life in 1864 as the Colorado Seminary. It was headquartered in downtown Denver in a building at 14th and Arapahoe streets. Founded by John Evans, a former governor of the Colorado Territory, the institution quickly succumbed to the harsh cycles of Colorado's economy. After four short years, a lack of funding forced Evans to close the institution's doors until 1880, when Colorado snapped out of its economic doldrums with the discovery of silver in the high country. The state's economic fortunes reversed course just as quickly, largely due to the silver panic of 1893. By that time, much of the institution had moved out of the noisy and smoky environs of downtown Denver to the site of today's campus. Evans was relieved as construction commenced and his long-awaited dream began to rise out of an empty landscape, on a site acquired by the university from a Colorado farmer, Rufus "Potato" Clark.

Thursday, April 3, 1890, dawned much the same as any other spring day in Colorado. At a festive ceremony attended by hundreds of university officials, trustees, and Denverites, Bishop Henry Warren hammered in University Hall's cornerstone. John Evans, then president of the board of trustees, joined numerous other dignitaries in giving rousing speeches. Beaming at the overflow crowd, Evans made a pronouncement that foreshadowed the university's role in the emerging city: "If you will look around you, you will see that the landscape extends far and wide in every direction, and that this institution, which is to rise upon this foundation, will be like a city set upon a hill that shall be known and seen by all men."

The university was fortunate to enlist the expertise of Colorado's first professional architect, Robert S. Roeschlaub, for the $80,000 project. Responsible for designing the institution's downtown academic buildings in the 1860s, as well as Denver's historic Trinity Church and the Central City Opera House, Roeschlaub utilized natural rock from the region to enhance University Hall's Richardsonian Romanesque architecture. Influenced by noted architect Henry Hobson Richardson (1838–1886), this style emphasized design elements on a grand scale, including the use of stone exteriors, low Roman archways, and grand staircases.

University archives indicate that the lava stone, or rhyolite, used for University Hall's exterior was quarried south of Denver near Castle Rock and then shipped via rail to the University Park campus. Because transportation options were few in those days, it was imperative in terms of time and

THESE THREE DOWNTOWN BUILDINGS, ALL
SINCE DEMOLISHED, ONCE HOUSED VARIOUS
UNIVERSITY ENTITIES—INCLUDING THE
MEDICAL AND PHARMACY PROGRAMS.
THESE SERVICEABLE STRUCTURES COULD
HAVE ADORNED ANY DOWNTOWN STREET
IN ANY MIDWESTERN CITY.

money to have building materials within close proximity. When installed, the rose-colored rhyolite gave a sense of strength and longevity; it also reflected the culture, values, and permanence of Colorado and the West. The original roof was most likely terra-cotta, a choice made to forestall the need for costly roof repairs.

The main entrance to University Hall features front doors framed by two stylized Corinthian columns. The entrance is centered on the building's south side and designated by a rising staircase, which is offset by two cylindrical half-towers with conical tops. These house the building's internal spiral staircases and reveal its circulation system to even the casual observer. Each of the towers is accessed from the outside by a short staircase. Two additional south-side entrances at garden level are set on either side of the main exterior staircase. The exterior is topped by a cupola that once sheltered a set of bells that summoned students and faculty to classes and chapel services. This tradition was discontinued during the 1940s.

Inside University Hall, Roeschlaub created hallways that run from end to end (east to west) on each of the building's four floors. These hallways connect the two oak staircases, which, in turn, connect the four floors. With their wide expanse and elegant but natural lines, these grand staircases epitomize the Richardsonian influence.

According to the December 18, 1891, edition of the university's newspaper, *The Hesperus*, the first floor held the chancellor's office, two reception rooms, a chapel, and two recital rooms. The second floor housed the university's growing library, with shelf space for more than 10,000 volumes, a reading room, a study hall, and four classrooms used for mathematics, literature, and the studies of Greek and Hebrew. The top floor housed the Evans Literary Club, Phi Alpha Society, and the offices of the school newspaper. It also included space built out for a future museum. Two additional rooms on this floor were created for "physical laboratories." Finally, the university's business offices, the girls' gymnasium, and a chemistry lab were all located on the garden level. As *The Hesperus* noted, "The interior is fully in keeping with the exterior, and the sense of freedom experienced by the surroundings. Nothing is cramped, and everything is planned on the same grand scale. No pains or money have been spared to secure every convenience."

On Monday, February 22, 1892, after two years of construction, University Hall opened its doors for the first time. The structure, draped in a large American flag and decorated with colorful bunting and DU colors, was an impressive sight to the 3,000 guests who came via railroad and horse-drawn carriages to witness this historic event. According to the March 2, 1892, edition of the *Colorado Transcript*, Bishop Warren drew enthusiastic applause with his remarks. "Some months ago, we laid in prayer and faith the cornerstone of this building. God only knows the importunateness of the prayer and the desperateness of the faith. Today we are shouting 'grace,' 'grace,' to the capstone in its beauty. The capstone of today is the cornerstone of tomorrow. The greatest we can do, the highest we can build, is only the foundation of what must be done."

That same year, Elizabeth Iliff Warren looked ahead to the future envisioned in that speech, pledging $100,000 for the construction of the Iliff School of Theology. From an architectural standpoint and land-use perspective, the new building was intended to complement University Hall. "The two buildings were meant to be seen as a pair, framing the view to the west, along with having their front doors aligned north to south. These buildings were essentially bookends," Mark Rodgers, current university architect, said.

Despite the relationship between the two buildings and despite the aspirations of Bishop Warren and Elizabeth Iliff Warren, the two institutions severed ties just five years later, largely because of financial issues. Thanks to mounting debts and an inadequate endowment, Elizabeth Warren closed Iliff in 1900, only to reopen it a decade later.

A NEW CENTURY DAWNS

The University of Denver's plans to expand its physical campus got a boost when Henry Augustus Buchtel began his twenty-one-year stint as chancellor in 1899. His resolve and ability to get things done were formidable, helping him contend with financial roadblocks occasioned by the 1893 silver panic and some monetary commitments to the school that never materialized.

Reportedly mortgaged to the hilt, in debt to the tune of about $200,000, and with faculty salaries unpaid for many months, the school's immediate future, let alone its long-term survival, was at stake. However, Buchtel nurtured a vision that cast the institution as a leader in higher education, and his tenure as chancellor is defined by the significant physical evolution of the campus.

Following the opening of University Hall, DU embarked on an ambitious building campaign, whose design motif and philosophy were modeled upon a variety of architectural precedents. At the behest of John Evans, Roeschlaub had established one of the school's earliest campus plans, creating

ARISING IN THE MIDDLE OF THE PLAINS, WITH NO ARCHITECTURAL CONTEXT TO DEFINE IT, THE EMERGING UNIVERSITY PARK CAMPUS DREW ON AMERICAN ARCHITECTURAL STYLES EMPLOYED IN OTHER REGIONS OF THE COUNTRY. ALTHOUGH THE TWO BUILDINGS— UNIVERSITY HALL AND THE ILIFF SCHOOL OF THEOLOGY—FACE EACH OTHER, THEY ARE SITED TO FRAME AN EXPANSIVE VIEW TO THE WEST.

UNIVERSITY HALL   No.298   UNIVERSITY LIBRARY

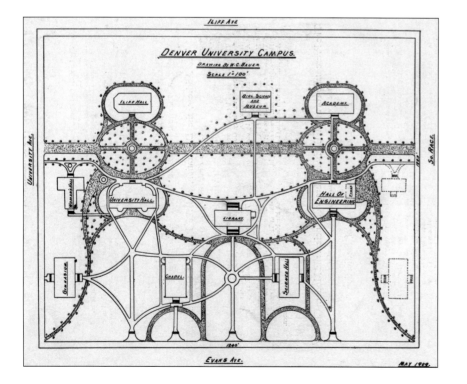

THE CARNEGIE LIBRARY, SHOWN ON THIS PAGE, ESTABLISHED A NEW ARCHITECTURAL STYLE ON CAMPUS. ITS NEOCLASSICAL DESIGN, TYPICAL OF MOST OF THE CARNEGIE LIBRARIES, SUGGESTS THAT THE UNIVERSITY'S LEADERSHIP WANTED TO ALIGN ITSELF WITH THE ARCHITECTURAL THINKING THEN CONSIDERED CUTTING EDGE. BY THEN, UNIVERSITY HALL'S RICHARDSONIAN ARCHITECTURE WAS REGARDED AS OUTDATED.

WHEN GROUND BROKE ON THE BUCHTEL MEMORIAL CHAPEL AND OLD SCIENCE HALL, SHOWN ON PAGE 17, UNIVERSITY LEADERS WERE LOOKING TO THE WEST — AND NOT TO THE EAST COAST — FOR ARCHITECTURAL INSPIRATION. THE BUCHTEL MEMORIAL CHAPEL WAS INSPIRED BY THE MISSION-STYLE ARCHITECTURE CHANCELLOR BUCHTEL ENCOUNTERED ON A TRIP TO CALIFORNIA. THE MASTER PLAN FROM THAT ERA PORTRAYS A CAMPUS THAT IS EXPANDING TO THE NORTH AND WEST.

a road map by which to position future buildings. One of the most notable characteristics of Roeschlaub's plan was that it maintained a strong view corridor to the west. Later, Buchtel updated the plan and added a series of quadrangles anchored by three buildings and open to the growing city of Denver to the north.

Buchtel presided over the construction of numerous facilities, including the Andrew S. Carnegie Library, Buchtel Memorial Chapel, Science Hall, and the Alumni Memorial Gymnasium. The Carnegie Library, situated between the current Penrose Library on the north and Mary Reed Building on the south, was the last of the 108 academic libraries personally funded by the famous industrialist. According to an article in the April 1990 edition of *American Libraries*, Carnegie funded construction of 1,670 libraries in 1,412 U.S. communities between 1889 and the mid-1920s. DU's library was initially funded with a $30,000 commitment from the Carnegie Foundation, with the proviso that the university match the amount.

Architectural historian Ellen C. Micaud, former associate professor in DU's School of Art and Art History, noted that the building was expected to serve as a landmark. "… It was intended as the centerpiece of the

new north [side of] campus. It fronted onto a planted quadrangle facing Evans, which was closed by Science Hall on the west and Buchtel Chapel on the east. It's essentially a pavilion, its prototype buildings essentially like the classical garden pavilions at Versailles," Micaud wrote in materials prepared for university tours.

Designed by Roeschlaub and his son, the library may not have reflected the architect's signature style, but as Micaud explained, it was a good example of neoclassical revival in its overall simplicity and harmonious design.

The one-story, cream-brick building, dedicated on September 7, 1909, featured seven expansive openings with rounded arches on the north and south facades. Three similar window openings were placed on the east and west sides, as well. University archives indicate that Ionic columns and pediment decorations utilizing terra-cotta, "with cartouches and acanthus leaves in each pediment," were all signatures of the design. The original interior featured fifteen rooms and approximately 9,600 square feet on the main floor and basement. The main floor's high ceilings, impressive beams, and large windows all combined to create a grand elegance.

After its use as a book repository was discontinued in the mid-1930s following the construction of the Mary Reed

Library, Carnegie Hall, as it was sometimes known, was modified numerous times for use as a student union, cafeteria, placement center, and bookstore. By 1990, it was the only remaining classically designed building on campus. It was torn down that year, after decades of deferred maintenance left it too dilapidated to renovate.

Andrew Carnegie's generosity did not stop with the library. Buchtel approached the philanthropist a second time in hopes of securing a grant to build a much-needed science building north and west of the library. Carnegie pledged $50,000, which the university then matched. Science Hall, affectionately known as the "Gas House," was constructed of a light-colored brick, similar to that used on Carnegie Library, and it served the DU community until it was demolished in 1996, after the opening of F.W. Olin Hall. The newly opened space, re-named Old Science Green, provided the critical link for the university's prime north-south promenade.

Despite its years of service, Science Hall was not greatly mourned. Although functional, its design failed aesthetically. As Micaud wrote, "The Science Building makes a gesture towards history, suggesting an Italian Renaissance villa with its four corner towers. However, the gesture is only that. The building is the clear result of an inadequate budget; it was an embarrassment to Roeschlaub, as well as a trial for those who worked in it all of these years."

In 1910, Alumni Gymnasium was built on the site of the present-day Daniels College of Business. Conforming with the other buildings constructed during this era, the Roeschlaub-designed structure incorporated features found in Roman or Renaissance architecture. The prototype for the building was the Roman Basilica. "The need was for a clear span, free as possible of cumbersome piers or columns, well lit from above," Micaud noted. During World War I, the gymnasium was converted into a barracks, housing close to 300 military personnel. Additionally, a hospital wing was constructed on the building's north side. That coincided with the dedication of the Buchtel Memorial Chapel, a tribute to the university's beloved chancellor—revered, in large part, because he rescued the institution from insolvency.

The cornerstone for the chapel had been laid in 1907, after Buchtel's return from a California vacation, when he purportedly handed Colorado Springs architect Thomas Barber a photograph of a mission-style church and asked him to create a similar-looking structure for the university. For a number of reasons, completing the facility proved to be a huge challenge. In fact, a full decade elapsed between groundbreaking and the building's official dedication. The chief reason for the delay was, not surprisingly, financing. Buchtel himself began raising support in 1907, and his enthusiasm for the project ignited the interest of the Colorado Conference of the Methodist Episcopal Church, which raised the $86,000 necessary to construct the chapel. Unfortunately, the funds came in piecemeal, so the building was constructed in like fashion.

For several years, the structure sat vacant without a roof, steps, or interior furnishings. Finally, in 1912, the University Chapel Guild was formed. Headed by Mrs. W.S. Iliff, the guild's mission was "to help in the completion of the chapel and to promote the social life of the [University] Park." University archives indicate the association's first order of business was to raise $1,350 for completion of the roof. Toward that end, guild members staged bake sales, rummage sales, fashion shows, parties, concerts, and community dinners. Buchtel then approached his good friend and Catholic benefactor, J.K. Mullen, for funds to complete the chapel's interior. Mullen generously agreed to the request, communicating his decision while Buchtel languished in his sick bed. Mullen's contribution raised the chancellor's spirits and reinforced his desire to give "hope that religious prejudices may vanish from the life of all Christian Bodies … ."

The chapel was sited between Science Hall and Alumni Gymnasium, just north and east of Carnegie Library. It featured exterior light brick with stone trim, a red tile roof, and four lofted, domed towers each covered in copper. The brick was specially manufactured to complete a color scheme of red and gold, by then the university's official colors. Its Spanish mission revival architecture was definitely out of context with the other structures around it, but it had its own charm nevertheless and represented one of the many Victorian revival styles then popular.

The church's interior was much admired, with ornate fixtures and other ecclesiastical paraphernalia. Two significant and valuable pieces included a thirty-two-pedal, electro-pneumatic pipe organ, given by Verner Z. Reed Jr., and a limited-edition framed replica of Raphael's Sistine Madonna, painted by copyist Herman Till. (Alas, the painting, as well as almost everything else inside the chapel, was lost when the structure burned to the ground in July 1983. The only remnant of the chapel still standing is a lone domed tower.)

ALONG WITH THE MASTER PLAN SHOWN
AT RIGHT, THIS AERIAL VIEW, CAPTURED
WELL BEFORE CONSTRUCTION BEGAN ON
MARGERY REED MAYO HALL, SHOWS A
CAMPUS ORIENTED TOWARD THE NORTH
AND DOWNTOWN DENVER. THE UNIVERSITY
WAS GROWING OUT TO GREET AND
EMBRACE THE CITY.

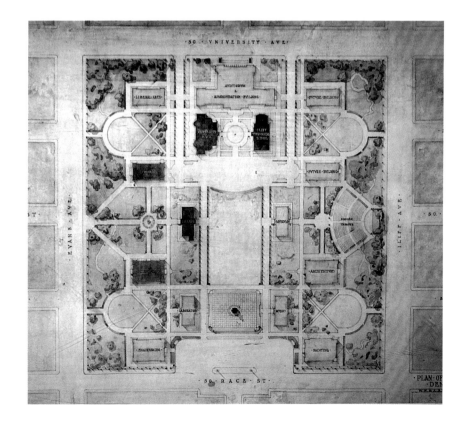

With the completion of the chapel, two of Buchtel's north-side open-ended quadrangles were complete. According to the campus plan from the end of this era, the south side of campus was intended to benefit from a similar set of quadrangles.

THE TWENTIES, THE DEPRESSION, AND WORLD WAR II

Following Buchtel's death in 1924, the university moved forward with expansion plans, albeit slowly. During the Depression and World War II, construction was limited, for obvious reasons, but in the Roaring Twenties, one prominent structure made its way off the drawing board: the DU football stadium. Among the first structures built north of Evans Avenue, the stadium was heavily promoted by William Seward Iliff (a team member in 1884) and partially funded by John Evans Jr., son of the university's founder. Tragically, during the 1946 homecoming football game, Iliff died of a heart attack in the stadium he helped bring to life.

The period also saw a new vision for the University Park campus inspired by the latest favored style: Collegiate Gothic. An ambitious campus map was prepared by Fisher and Fisher Architects. Fisher and Fisher collaborated with Charles Z. Klauder, a Philadelphia-based architect known nationally for his work on university campuses. This plan provided for campus growth to the north and south of the original block of land. It also showed a series of closed quadrangles framing an east-west view as well as a new north-south axis connecting the academic buildings to the football stadium. In addition, the plan provided for construction of a row of fraternities and, shockingly, the demolition of both University Hall and the Carnegie Library. By doing so, the plan essentially dismissed the architectural styles that had prevailed previously.

While many of the buildings envisioned during this era were shelved due to financial constraints, two architecturally significant buildings were constructed in the late twenties into the early thirties. Margery Reed Mayo Hall was completed in 1928, followed by the Mary Reed Library four years later.

In November 1926, Mrs. Verner Z. Reed, a DU trustee and patron, told Chancellor Heber Reece Harper, who served from 1922 to 1927, that she wanted to commit $100,000 for the construction of a building to honor her late daughter, Margery Reed Mayo, DU class of 1919. Assisted by Fisher and Fisher Architects, Klauder was hired to create Margery

EVANS CHAPEL

"Few landmarks which reflect the precious past of a region are held in greater esteem by its people than a historic place of worship."
FORMER CHANCELLOR CHESTER M ALTER DISCUSSING EVANS CHAPEL

Evans Chapel was constructed in 1878, its $13,000 cost funded by DU founder John Evans in honor of his daughter, Josephine, who had died a decade earlier. The chapel was originally built as an addition to Grace Methodist Episcopal Church, which stood at the corner of 13th and Bannock streets in downtown Denver.

In 1958, after the church moved to a new home at a different location, the University of Denver purchased the property, including the Evans Chapel. Some DU officials openly considered demolishing the chapel to make room for parking, but Chester Alter and John Evans, grandson of the chapel's benefactor, saved it from the wrecking ball. After Evans donated the necessary funds, the building was moved to the University Park campus and situated on a direct axis between what was then the Mary Reed Library and Mount Evans. Today it stands serenely at what has become the busiest crossroads of campus.

Because it was impossible to transport the 400-ton stone chapel intact, the building was dismantled by hand, stone by stone and window by window. Each piece was carefully numbered so that the chapel could be reassembled almost as it was.

On June 10, 1960, the Evans Memorial Chapel was rededicated. Today, the nondenominational chapel is a popular choice for personal prayer and meditation, as well as for weddings and baptisms. It also serves as a tangible reminder of the university's early history.

Reed Mayo Hall, which officially opened in fall 1928. Some years later, the name of the building was shortened to Margery Reed Hall.

Located near Alumni Gymnasium and the Buchtel Memorial Chapel, the liberal arts structure was the first building on campus designed in the Collegiate Gothic style. The building, which cost $256,000, featured sixteen classrooms, faculty offices, and a 300-person theater. Noted Denver artist John E. Thompson painted an exquisite mural of Shakespearean characters in the theater in 1929. Just eighteen months after the building's debut, the mural was painted over and only rediscovered in 2006.

In June 1927, *The Denver Post* praised the building's style. "Simplicity and dignity are the keynotes of the Collegiate Gothic form … with attention to that quality of grandeur which seems to be rooted in spirituality." Chancellor Harper and the trustees decided all future buildings at DU would be designed in the same style, which reigned through the construction of the Mary Reed Building and the old row fraternities.

After only two decades, Carnegie Library had outgrown its walls, so university officials decided to build a new library. Just west of University Hall, the Mary Reed Library (today known as the Mary Reed Building) officially opened in January 1933 and cost $350,000. Once again, Mrs. Verner Z. Reed contributed the necessary funds, and as a result, the building bears her name. Denver architect Harry J. Manning oversaw design. Manning was no novice. According to Micaud, he was "an acknowledged master in the art of adapting historical styles to modern purposes."

According to architectural consultant Bill Campbell, the Mary Reed Building's orientation creates "maximum perimeter exposure," which was especially true when few trees or vegetation existed. From atop the observation deck on its 126-foot tower, visitors can see the entire Front Range, from Pikes Peak to the south to Longs Peak to the north. University archives suggest the building, whose stacks could hold more than 400,000 volumes, was specifically designed in an "H" pattern, thereby allowing the three major reference and study halls to catch natural light from the north, south, and west. The building was constructed of a reinforced concrete facade with dark, rose-colored brick accented and trimmed with Indiana limestone.

The interior included spacious reading rooms, customized furniture designed by the building's architect, numerous exhibit rooms for archaeology and art displays, mullioned bay windows, wrought-iron railings with aluminum caps, exhibit cases, and a distinctive clustering

of cathedral lights. These details made the Mary Reed Library a DU and Denver landmark. To this day, the stately structure is considered one of the university's signature buildings.

The location of the building, however, reveals how quickly campus-planning ideals were evolving. The 1930 Fisher and Fisher plan located the new library where the Daniels College of Business now stands, leaving the top of the hill between University Hall and the Iliff School of Theology building vacant. This plan maintained an unobstructed view to the west, one framed by the two stone buildings. By 1933, that priority gave way to a Jeffersonian ideal—implemented at the University of Virginia—that placed the university library at the heart of campus and on the highest ground.

While the effects of the Depression and World War II precluded thoughts of significant expansion on the University Park campus, such was not the case for the downtown campus. During Chancellor Ben Cherrington's tenure from 1943 to 1946, DU acquired an entire block across from Civic Center Park for the School of Commerce. The acquisition was made possible largely through the efforts of trustee and United States National Bank President Thomas Dines, who saw the link between a vibrant metropolis and a dynamic institution of higher learning. Said Dines, "You can't have a great city without a great university."

Still another master plan, this one authored in 1947, proposed new buildings for engineering and arts and sciences, as well as a speech clinic, dormitories, a new gymnasium, and an administration building. This plan called for construction in a modern style, a significant departure from the Collegiate Gothic. Noted Denver architect Burnham Hoyt, who designed the Denver Public Library, was slated to design a $500,000 student union and cafeteria, just part of a $15 million makeover intended to bring the campus into the automobile age. The plan emphasized highway access to the campus and, for the first time, parking needs. Those plans never materialized. Instead, the university broke ground on several utilitarian dormitories, needed to house the influx of soldiers returning from World War II.

PLANNING FOR THE FUTURE

The early 1950s saw limited building, largely because of financial considerations and an emphasis on developing educational programs and building the endowment. In fact, no new buildings were constructed between 1950 and 1956. However, as enrollment increased with postwar prosperity, the need for on-campus housing grew accordingly. Consequently, in the latter part of the 1950s, construction resumed. Johnson-McFarlane Hall was built for $1.7 million, and ground was broken for a new downtown University Law Center at 14th and Bannock streets in 1959. The trustees and Chancellor Chester Alter, in office from 1953 to 1966, enlisted the design firm of Perkins & Will Architects Engineers to guide DU in putting together a comprehensive plan for future facilities. Curiously, university archives are overflowing with interesting but never implemented design plans from this era.

The plans that did come to fruition called for yet another departure from previous architectural styles. The Boettcher Center for Science, Engineering, and Research opened in the early 1960s to rave reviews. Still in use today, this concrete structure's architectural style, labeled International, was counter to anything built on campus to that point. While innovative in its use of space and planning, Boettcher's precast concrete facade and modern look lacked the style and charm of earlier buildings.

Perkins & Will continued its favored style with 1964's Centennial Halls and Towers and 1966's Cherrington Hall, home to the Graduate School of International Studies, renamed the Josef Korbel School of International Studies in 2008. The firm followed with the Business Administration Building in 1968 and the General Classroom Building (now Sturm Hall) a year later.

By 1972, Penrose Library, considered state-of-the-art at the time, opened its doors in the heart of the campus. The noted architectural firm H.O.K. designed Penrose as a machine for learning devoid of decoration. It was accompanied by yet another master plan, this one calling for multiple buildings in the newest style, with the intention of overwhelming the buildings from earlier eras.

Such was the campus that, in the late 1980s and early 1990s, stood poised for the coming millennium: a hodgepodge of architectural styles, a host of buildings constructed to deal with immediate problems, and a handful of discordant gems from eras gone by.

When Daniel L. Ritchie assumed the chancellor's post in 1989, the University of Denver faced a precarious financial situation and a number of sizable infrastructure issues. Chief among them were the tasks of readying old buildings for new challenges, of developing structures tailored to 21st century needs, of blending the disparate textures and styles to create an inspirational place for thinking and learning.

CONSTRUCTED IN THE COLLEGIATE GOTHIC STYLE, MARGERY REED MAYO HALL WAS DESIGNED BY CHARLES KLAUDER, ONE OF THE NATION'S LEADING CAMPUS ARCHITECTS. KLAUDER'S INVOLVEMENT IN THE PROJECT SUGGESTS THAT, ONCE AGAIN, THE INSTITUTION'S LEADERSHIP WAS TAKING ITS CUES AND VISION FROM THE EASTERN STATES.

OVER THE YEARS, MARGERY REED MAYO HALL BECAME A CULTURAL RESOURCE FOR THE COMMUNITY, LARGELY THANKS TO ITS THEATER, WHOSE DESIGN REFERENCES ELIZABETHAN ENGLAND. THE COLLEGIATE GOTHIC STYLE, WITH ITS NOD TO THE RENAISSANCE AND TO EUROPEAN TRADITIONS, WAS HUGELY POPULAR ON UNIVERSITY CAMPUSES IN THE FIRST DECADES OF THE TWENTIETH CENTURY.

CHARLES Z KLAUDER · REG ARCH
FISHER & FISHER – ASSOCIATES

1429 WALNUT ST – PHILADELPHIA

MAR · 2 · 1928 – SCALE ⅛" = 1'-0"

WORK No. 996 A
DRAWING No. Sk B 2.

· ROOF PLAN OF AUDITORIUM ·

PRELIMINARY DRAWING

23

THE MARY REED LIBRARY WAS DESIGNED TO ANCHOR THE CAMPUS
AND EVEN TO TOWER OVER THE OTHER BUILDINGS. BECAUSE OF ITS
ROLE AS AN INFORMATION REPOSITORY, ITS LOCATION AT THE
HEART OF CAMPUS SIGNALED THAT THE UNIVERSITY OF DENVER
WAS A SERIOUS INSTITUTION OF HIGHER LEARNING.

CONSTRUCTION ON THE MARY REED LIBRARY WAS COMPLETED
DURING THE DEPRESSION. THE ORNATE STONE- AND BRICKWORK
MADE THE PROJECT TIME- AND LABOR-INTENSIVE.

COLLEGIATE GOTHIC ARCHITECTURE
BORROWS MOTIFS FROM AND PAYS
TRIBUTE TO COLLEGES IN ENGLAND.
THE FIRST FLOOR OF THE MARY REED
LIBRARY SHOWCASES THE ELABORATE
FENESTRATION AND STONE ARCHES
CHARACTERISTIC OF THE STYLE.

IN THE YEARS FOLLOWING
WORLD WAR II, THE MARY
REED LIBRARY REMAINED
THE FOCAL POINT OF
CAMPUS, THOUGH THE NEW
BUILDINGS THAT EMERGED
AROUND IT DEPARTED
RADICALLY FROM THE
COLLEGIATE GOTHIC.

THE BOETTCHER CENTER,
ABOVE, REFERENCED THE
INTERNATIONAL STYLE OF
ARCHITECTURE, CHARACTER-
IZED BY SQUARE OR
RECTANGULAR FOOTPRINTS
AND EXTENSIVE USE OF
REINFORCED CONCRETE.
IN THIS RENDERING, THE
BUILDING FEATURES EXTRA
WINGS THAT WERE NEVER
CONSTRUCTED. LIKE THE
BOETTCHER CENTER, BEN
CHERRINGTON HALL, SHOWN
AT LEFT, FEATURES A STRONG
VERTICAL GRID ON A
HORIZONTAL STRUCTURE.

THE DRISCOLL CENTER, BUILT
IN 1982, ADOPTED THE
ARCHITECTURAL STYLE
PREVALENT ON COLLEGE
CAMPUSES AT THE TIME. AS
UNIVERSITY ARCHITECT
MARK RODGERS NOTED, "DU
IS STILL TELLING THE WORLD
THAT IT IS RIDING THE WAVE."
WHEN FIRST CONSTRUCTED,
PENROSE LIBRARY, SHOWN AT
RIGHT, WAS CLEARLY TRYING
TO EDGE OUT OLD SCIENCE
HALL, ITS NEIGHBOR TO THE
EAST. OLD SCIENCE HALL
WAS LATER DEMOLISHED.

BUILT IN 1925, THE FOOTBALL STADIUM HAD SEATING
CAPACITY FOR 26,000 SPECTATORS, MAKING IT A RESOURCE
FOR THE ENTIRE COMMUNITY. UNTIL IT WAS TORN DOWN
IN 1971, THE STADIUM HOSTED EVENTS ENJOYED BY
COLORADANS FROM ALL WALKS OF LIFE.

By the 1990s, the University of Denver campus was long overdue for some tender loving care. It was also in dire need of new facilities — buildings that could enhance its viability as a 21st century pioneer in higher education. The challenge facing the transformation team was staggering: How do you create a cohesive and dynamic learning environment from disparate architectural styles, from buildings constructed to address short-term needs? How do you honor the past while servicing the present and endowing the future? How do you create a campus that could only belong to the University of Denver?

SHAPING A CAMPUS FOR THE 21ST CENTURY

2

"*The architecture of a university's campus is an open book that most of us have forgotten how to read. The ways that buildings relate to each other, and to the environment in which they are set, communicate meaning, character, and significance.*"

— ALLAN GREENBERG, Author/Architect

THE CHALLENGE FACING ARCHITECT CAB CHILDRESS, SHOWN ABOVE, AND CHANCELLOR DAN RITCHIE, LEFT, WAS FORMIDABLE: CREATE A CAMPUS WHERE THE NEW ARCHITECTURE WOULD MAKE THE OLDER STRUCTURES LOOK BETTER. TODAY, FROM THE BUCHTEL TOWER TO THE WILLIAMS TOWER, THE CAMPUS BLENDS OLD AND NEW SEAMLESSLY.

By the early 1980s, the University of Denver was coming face to face with the size and scope of its simmering challenges — precarious finances, declining enrollment, and a deteriorating physical campus.

For Daniel Ritchie, chancellor of the university from 1989 to 2005, updating and reinvigorating the physical campus was, in many respects, priority number one. After all, if he was to strengthen the university's financial situation, the institution needed a stable enrollment. To lure students to the school and to secure its reputation, it needed buildings that testified to the quality of the learning experience within.

Ritchie brought to this task a handful of goals and stipulations. The campus should express the aspirations and values of the institution and not the genius of a select group of "name" architects. Any new buildings should incorporate materials that would withstand the ravages of time, weather, and use. Just as important, these buildings should welcome and delight; they should stimulate learning and foster collaboration. Finally, they should symbolize the university's comeback, its stature within the city, state, and nation.

Perhaps Jim Griesemer, the former chief financial officer of the university who later served as dean of the Daniels College of Business, put it best: "Because measuring the value of an education is inherently difficult due to its intangible nature, one ends up using metaphors to convey quality. At DU, distinctive buildings were our metaphor for conveying a superior educational experience."

TACKLING THE LONG-DEFERRED CHALLENGES

Throughout the 1980s, the university's shaky financial condition undermined its ability to perform at peak. Longtime university trustee Joy Burns remembers that the institution's leaders faced some painfully tough decisions. "I came on the board in 1981, and by 1982, we [the trustees] came to realize we were in desperate shape financially, as enrollment projections were way off for two years in a row," Burns said. "Additionally, there was about $60 million in deferred maintenance. Our facilities were not in very good shape." Ritchie, who joined the board a year later, went so far as to call the situation "embarrassing."

According to Griesemer, the university found itself in constrained circumstances because of three converging factors. First, the university acquired the Colorado Women's College (CWC), located on what became the Park Hill campus, in the early 1980s and took on the significant

maintenance costs and debt associated with the facilities. Following the CWC acquisition, DU built the Lowell Thomas Law Center on the Park Hill campus, moving the law school from its downtown Denver location. And finally, the university raised faculty salaries and increased its operating expenditures.

In 1985 and 1986, the financial crunch was aggravated by continued slides in enrollment, resulting in an operating deficit of roughly $8 million to $9 million. "For a private university which was 80 percent tuition dependent," Griesemer said, "it had moved itself, wittingly or unwittingly, into an extremely precarious position — a classic 'tipping point' phenomenon."

Still another problem grew out of the fiscal model, in which revenues were calculated and managed centrally, while expenditures were managed in a decentralized fashion. In other words, the school's central administration approved expenditures and department budgets, but the management of those budgets resided with the deans of each school. When revenues went down, there was no system in place to alert the people spending money.

After taking stock of this situation, the administration implemented an incentive-based budgeting system, whereby the deans of each school were not only responsible for spending and allocating their program's budget resources, they were charged with accounting for it, as well. The deans reaped financial benefits for their programs based on how much money they brought in and how carefully they managed their budgets. These systems and structures gave each dean more autonomy and cast the leadership in an entrepreneurial role.

For example, if a dean generated more revenue than projected in his or her annual budget, the program could keep fifty percent of the overage, while DU kept the remaining fifty percent. Savings on the expenditure side were also managed differently. "If you underspent your budget," Griesemer said, "you were allowed to keep 100 percent of what you didn't spend. These funds were put in a special account that the department could use with considerable discretion. Before the gain-sharing system was established, departments would *lose* 100 percent of any unspent funds. Not surprisingly, they spent every cent in their budgets. After the establishment of the gain-sharing system, the changes in behavior were just unbelievable." In fact, just five months after the new model's implementation, the departments emerged from deficit spending and created a budget surplus of about $700,000.

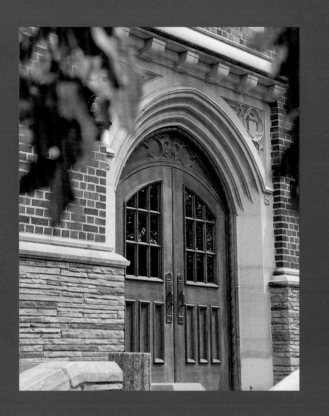

MARY REED BUILDING
DOORS

Architect Cab Childress knew that small changes can make big differences.

Early in the process of re-imagining the University Park campus, Childress and trustee Joy Burns had a conversation about sprucing up the Mary Reed Building. "If you could do anything you want to, what would it be?" Burns asked Childress.

Childress perused the Collegiate Gothic structure carefully, from its intricately carved limestone trim to its mullioned windows. And then his eyes fell on the doors. Ugly metal doors. Gymnasium doors. Doors that belonged on another building from another era.

"Replace those doors," Childress said. Burns, always one to trust Childress' prescriptions, had a reply at the ready: "Do it! I'll pay for it!"

And so the painted metal doors came down and in their place a set of beautiful wooden panels was installed. Each panel was lovingly finished to match the time-tested wooden shelves and fixtures inside the building.

For Childress, doors represented a visitor's first contact with a building. Getting the right door set the tone for the relationship to come.

As the university was addressing its fiscal challenges, it was also reviewing its construction and maintenance priorities. Science Hall, Alumni Gymnasium, and Carnegie Library, all venerable facilities, were in dire need of repairs and renovations, as were a host of other buildings. Griesemer vividly remembers a site visit to Carnegie Library with the late Al Cohen of Cohen Construction, a longtime trustee and then chairman of the university's building and grounds committee. "Al took a wood pencil out of his shirt pocket and pushed it through the mortar and brick until it came out the other side. He then looked at me and said, 'We have some problems.'"

As it turned out, that was a massive understatement.

ADDRESSING THE PROBLEMS—
SYSTEMATICALLY AND ASSERTIVELY

As the 1980s came to a close, DU found itself in need of a leader who could capitalize on its recent gains, negotiate its business challenges, and spearhead new initiatives. The trustees did not need to look far for the institution's next chancellor. Daniel Ritchie was sitting at their table.

Ritchie, who had joined the board in 1983 and who had previously served as CEO of Westinghouse Broadcasting, was well liked by his fellow trustees. Just as important, he was trusted. "In addition to the fact Dan is absolutely one of the best fundraisers I shall ever know, he is also a man of integrity," Joy Burns said. "You just know that something good is going to happen with your money. Somehow, you just cannot say no to that man."

Ritchie wasted no time in getting to work, shoring up the institution's financial house and putting key people in critical positions. The job of identifying and prioritizing current and future building needs proved an especially daunting task. In looking back on the state of DU's campus infrastructure at the time, Ritchie remembers a grim scene characterized by deterioration. "You didn't think in terms of potential because what was required was so massive," he said.

One of Ritchie's first steps was to call for a disciplined approach to long-term planning. Like many colleges and universities around the country, DU had grown accustomed to embarking on initiatives and building projects that were unaligned with a larger strategic vision. At DU, for example, numerous living quarters had been constructed to accommodate returning troops from World War II, but little thought had been given to how and where they were built.

When it came time to break ground, any campus green space was fair game for construction. And by the time Ritchie became chancellor, the university's prior leadership had already shelved numerous land-use plans. As university architect Mark Rodgers aptly pointed out, there were "many grand revisions as opposed to grand visions."

The initial phase of the university's 1994 plan called for construction of three new buildings — one for science, one for business, and one for athletics and recreation. It also provided for the renovation of University Hall and an addition to the Ricks Center for Gifted Children. In time, as the emerging needs of a resurgent DU became clearer, the plan was modified to allow for additional construction.

The evolving plan also served to address concerns from the nearby neighborhoods. As the university broke ground on new buildings, and as its changing fortunes resulted in an influx of new students to the campus, the neighbors grew concerned that a rejuvenated DU would compromise their quality of life. New structures and new students meant traffic jams, parking shortages, and increased noise. Throughout the next few years, DU would use its plan to anticipate and mitigate the effects of its projects on the neighbors. That meant adding parking spaces and structures, scaling buildings to complement the neighborhoods, and introducing programs to sensitize the university community to neighbor concerns.

Fortunately, Ritchie was no stranger to the many challenges associated with construction, having learned about the business during an earlier stint with MCA, when he had helped develop Universal City in Hollywood. By 1993 Ritchie had come to the conclusion that it would be necessary to plan for at least four or five new buildings. To Ritchie's mind, the project needed a lead architect, someone with the requisite expertise, a design philosophy in sync with the high-minded mission of a university, and a keen desire to create beautiful buildings that serve human needs.

Enter G. Cabell Childress. A long-practicing Denver-based architect, Childress — known as Cab — had an impressive list of exquisite Colorado projects to his credit, including the Eagle County government building, the Evergreen Public Library, and the dance and theater building at the University of Colorado. By the time Ritchie contacted Childress about projects at DU, the latter had been casting about for a meaty project to cap and close his career.

Ritchie first met Childress in 1980 after a referral from *The Denver Post's* architectural writer, Joanne Ditmer. Ritchie had been looking for an architect to assist him in building a main house at his Grand River Ranch outside of Kremmling, Colorado. Ditmer gave him a short list of reputable architects —with Childress' name at the top of that list.

During the course of their collaboration on the ranch, Ritchie and Childress developed a working style that suited each. They also discovered that they shared many of the same ideas about architecture and place, about the Colorado landscape, and about the role of buildings in fostering culture and community. "There was," Jim Griesemer explained, "no daylight between them."

Childress was initially hired in 1992 to craft the design of a new outdoor plaza. At the time, he was one of several architects tackling university projects. By fall 1992, Ritchie had sought his advice on a new athletic center, and within the next year, offered him the position of university architect. Childress was asked to look at the entire campus as his canvas.

What made Childress the man for the job? In an interview in summer 2006, just months before he died, Childress explained that, in many ways, his entire career had paved the way for this assignment. He had begun his practice in a humble setting, taking small assignments and giving them his best. "When you start a practice, you have to build with wood and cheap materials. And each time you go, you get a little bit better and a little bit better and a little bit better," he recalled.

Year after year, all the while getting a bit better and a bit better, he'd worked on the University of Colorado Design Review Board, taught for a time at DU's School of Art and Art History, and created a host of churches, homes, and public buildings for Colorado. Finally, he was ready for a client who would demand not better, but best.

For Childress, the call from Ritchie had almost mystical overtones. Looking back on their collaboration, he noted that he and Ritchie shared generational and geographical mindsets. Born just a few months apart, they were Southerners from a can-do generation, men who put a lot of stock in their convictions. "Cab was honest, spoke his mind, and wasn't going to be stymied by anyone, including Dan. I think Dan loved that about Cab, even though he knew they might butt heads once in a while," Mark Rodgers said.

In addition to his philosophical compatibility with Ritchie, Childress was an uncompromising advocate for quality. He believed, like Ritchie, that buildings were more than warehouses and workspaces, that a good building should provide the setting for memories and the flowering of human creativity. He also believed that buildings should engage their inhabitants in a discovery process, that they

ALUMNI GYMNASIUM, BUILT IN 1910, WAS
IMPLODED IN SEPTEMBER 1997 TO MAKE WAY
FOR THE DANIELS COLLEGE OF BUSINESS.
MANY OF ITS MATERIALS WERE SALVAGED
FOR RECYCLING.

CHILDRESS AND RITCHIE ENJOYED A RELATIONSHIP
SOLIDIFIED BY A COMMON VISION. BOTH WANTED
TO CONSTRUCT BUILDINGS THAT WOULD BELONG
TO COLORADO AND THAT WOULD WITHSTAND
THE TESTS OF TIME.

would reveal their character and personality over time. With that in mind, Childress thought about how his buildings would cast shadows and how they would settle into their sites. Just as important, he looked ahead to how the building would age, not just decades from groundbreaking, but centuries. Any architect worth his fee, Childress insisted, would strive to build a good ruin.

Childress was also an indefatigable student. He studied and analyzed every aspect of a job, researching all possible design alternatives. Ever the information sponge, he pursued knowledge relentlessly, studying, in the case of DU, its history and traditions. He also had an innate understanding of how different building materials—brick and limestone, sandstone and copper—interact with one another and influence the overall design concept. Finally, he was sensitive to how buildings relate to one another, how they combine to create harmony or clash to foster discord.

Rodgers, who collaborated at the same design table with his mentor throughout the 1990s, believes that Childress' acute sense of context helped him envision the campus as a whole, even when looking years down the road. "I think one of the reasons that Dan picked Cab was because he was exceptional at taking what was in place and making it better, as opposed to putting something in place and then hoping the rest of the campus would catch up," Rodgers explained. "…Cab was just a tenacious, phenomenal architect when it came to dealing with site and context."

On April Fools' Day of 1994, Childress began work as university architect, ready to tackle the priorities articulated by Ritchie and championed by the university's buildings and grounds committee, chaired by trustee Patricia Livingston. The forthcoming buildings would be constructed with quality materials and first-rate craftsmanship. They would be built to last, to stand and serve for hundreds of years. For a model, Ritchie pointed to the University of Bologna in Italy, purportedly the oldest university in the western world. Many of the beautifully executed buildings there are close to 900 years old, and as Ritchie was fond of noting, no one would ever dream of tearing them down. "And that was our idea," Ritchie said. "Buildings built of stone and built to last, from the copper roofs down to the foundations, as well as not being something that's expendable in twenty-five to fifty years. For us, it's a philosophy of quality and honesty that these buildings need to express."

Childress added his own twist to this view. "Cab said you should be able to look at a building and smile," Ritchie recalled. "And if you don't smile, then we have failed. I also

believed Cab would lavish the most important ingredient in any building on his DU project: love."

BREAKING GROUND ON A LABOR OF LOVE

Before large-scale construction could begin, it was critical that Ritchie educate DU's alumni, faculty, and friends about the university's plans and that he secure the board of trustees' blessing to court donors. From the beginning, he was confident that his scheme to build for posterity would resonate with DU's core constituencies and Colorado's philanthropic community. His credo was simple: "Money follows quality and not the other way around."

To reassure the board that spending would not outpace fundraising, Ritchie stipulated that the university would live within its budget. This commitment was adopted by every academic, athletic, and administrative entity within DU. For the team masterminding the institution's transformation, this meant that no building project moved forward until at least 80 percent of the money needed to complete the facility was firmly committed. In some cases, that number was 100 percent.

According to Griesemer, Ritchie's insistence on quality and fiscal responsibility sent a powerful message to donors. "People were very willing to pay for quality," he explained. "It connoted educational performance was a long-term value at DU and not a transitory one."

Once potential donors understood the magnitude of the new plans, once they realized what the end result would mean not only to DU but also to the city and state, they *wanted* to be involved. Their financial commitment to the university marked a significant turning point in the institution's fortunes. Ritchie himself was one of the first to step up and contribute funds, selling a portion of his Grand River Ranch to do so. The university's financial picture was made even rosier in 2003, when the institution completed the sale of the final parcel of land at its Park Hill campus to Johnson & Wales University. The resulting infusion of cash was put to use when DU began construction of its new law facility on the University Park campus.

With the money beginning to roll in, Childress got right to work. John Prosser, chairman of the University of Colorado's Design Review Board, likened his friend's work to a brain-teasing encounter with a chessboard. Collaborating with Ritchie, Childress strategically placed each new building in the best possible site, integrating the new structures with

OVER THE DECADES, THE UNIVERSITY OF DENVER CAMPUS HAS ADDED BUILDINGS,
RESHAPED ITS GROUNDS, AND EVOLVED INTO A DYNAMIC LEARNING COMMUNITY,
AS WELL AS A VITAL RESOURCE FOR THE CITY AND STATE.

the fixed pieces, positioning them so they complemented the surrounding campus. As he saw it, the university represented a village, a bustling community that needed areas for quiet work, for sharing meals, for celebrating and recreating.

Deciding on locations, choosing materials, and formulating design concepts, Ritchie and Childress began to stitch together a campus tapestry. From Rodgers' vantage point as apprentice and team player, the operation was an instructive and inspiring lesson in collaboration. "It was definitely not a situation where Cab led Dan or Dan led Cab," he recalled. "Those two did a dance that was just amazing to watch."

To create a cohesive identity for the university, Ritchie and Childress looked to the existing buildings on campus for guidance, particularly the Mary Reed Building. With its Collegiate Gothic design and harmonious blend of brick and stone, the building had not only aged gracefully, it had retained its sense of dignity and purpose. It was attractive and solid, worthy of its landmark status—all without seeming overbearing or outdated.

Determined that their new buildings would enhance their context, Ritchie and Childress chose timeless materials that testified to the colors and textures in Colorado's landscape: red brick and mortar, rosy sandstone, Indiana limestone, and copper. "Nothing ages faster than trendy," Childress said, eschewing materials and designs that might have been deemed cutting-edge or innovative. Childress also drew upon building practices from an earlier era, bringing in craftsmen and artisans with Old World sensibilities and a New World attitude toward problem solving. He called for double-wall brick construction, ensuring that his buildings would be able to withstand the trials of time and the tribulations of weather.

In planning the interior spaces, Childress and Ritchie opted for flexible spaces that could adapt to changing times, support state-of-the-art technology, bring people together, and relate to the outdoors. Just as important, they left room for art and architectural details, for unexpected treasures that lift the human spirit.

On the other side of windows and entries, Childress and Ritchie envisioned a landscape that suited a Westerner's hankering for wide, open spaces, that addressed the human need for connection, and that provided an inspirational setting for learning. "I've always been interested in human space and figuring out what makes it so inviting, or repelling, for that matter," Ritchie explained. "Without it being too symmetrical, I'm interested in how things line up and center. The environment, with buildings that support our students, makes a huge difference in learning."

Within no time, ground was broken on the first three buildings to emerge from Childress' creative beehive: F. W. Olin Hall, the Daniel L. Ritchie Center for Sports & Wellness, and the Daniels College of Business. As construction proceeded on these buildings, design began on a host of others. Soon, the university had more than 500,000 square feet of new space either underway or on the drawing boards. Construction cranes were as ubiquitous as students. A new University of Denver was in the making.

CAB
CHILDRESS

Throughout his professional life, architect G. Cabell Childress worked to build a great wall.

As he defined it, a great wall will stand for centuries. It will adapt to the times, respond to new needs, and withstand the elements. Ultimately, it will make a graceful ruin, a reminder of eras gone by.

By the time he died at age 74 in November 2006, Childress had built walls aplenty. None of them are ruins yet, and so none of them can yet be called great. But Childress' walls are certainly off to an auspicious start, providing a worthy backdrop for all manner of human endeavor.

Born on March 13, 1932, in Bristol, Virginia, Childress practiced a brand of architecture dedicated to human endeavor. His buildings were meant to be used and loved. They were meant, he once said, "to recognize nature, honor the past, and endow the future."

He grew up in Tampa, Florida, and earned a bachelor of science degree in architectural engineering from the Georgia Institute of Technology. After graduating, he was commissioned in the Navy and assigned to the Atlantic and Mediterranean destroyer fleets. He left the Navy in 1957 and moved with his wife, Penelope Frances Nace, to Boulder, where he completed a year of postgraduate study in architecture at the University of Colorado. Subsequently, he joined the Denver firm of W.C. Muchow and taught at the University of Denver and the University of Colorado.

Childress launched his own firm—Cabell Childress Architects—in 1966. Over the years, as he and his wife raised their four children and traveled the world, he took on hundreds of design projects: churches, corporate buildings, renovations, additions, park facilities, a home for his family, and a studio for his work. By the end of his career, he was known not only for his achievements at the University of Denver, but also for the Eagle County Government Center, the visitors center at Roxborough State Park, the Evergreen Public Library, and the University of Colorado Theatre and Dance Building. Thanks to his work on the latter, Childress was elected to the prestigious CU Design Review Board, established in 1968 to ensure that the Boulder campus maintains its architectural character.

In Boulder, Childress developed a lasting friendship with architect John Prosser, current head of the Design Review Board and a trusted advisor on the University of Denver projects. Prosser marveled over the many influences Childress brought to his work. "Cab's design philosophy was really enhanced because of his photographic memory," Prosser said. "He traveled extensively, and his ability to recall various buildings' details and put them into context was so incisive. He was so incredibly creative."

In all his commissions, Childress insisted on respect for context and for the past. As an aspiring architect romanced by the possibilities of modernism, he initially dismissed the work of earlier eras. "I was taught to hate anything old and love anything avant-garde," he told an interviewer in summer 2006. "I came to my senses in college."

Throughout his career, Childress was happy to learn from the masters, whether they built cathedrals in France or temples in Japan. "I operate on the basis that I would rather steal something good than produce something poor," he said. A scrupulous archivist, he kept drawings, photos, and notes on buildings and graphics that he admired. His ten-volume hand-lettered memoir, *Cabell's Wonderous Voyage Through the Twentieth Century*, the original of which he donated to the Denver Public Library's Western History and Genealogy Collection, chronicles the quotidian and the esoteric—everything from his start-up years in private practice to his love affair with a quarry floor tile known as Heather Brown.

Childress' maverick and immersive approach to architecture often put him at loggerheads with others in the design community. While teaching at the University of Colorado at Denver, he clashed with colleagues who questioned his philosophical direction. One of Childress' students at the time was Bill Campbell, who now serves the University of Denver as an architectural consultant. "Cab was bumping heads with the administration, who were trying to teach 'style,' and Cab was definitely anti-style. I remember him saying to our class, 'Let's learn appropriate Colorado architecture,'" Campbell said.

Childress' reverence for context translated into an eccentric methodology. As Campbell remembers it, Childress would send his apprentice architects to a project site to study it throughout the course of a day. They would watch how the sun hit the site, where the shadows fell, how the wind stirred the vegetation. On sites like DU, where new buildings were expected to interact with old, Childress would instruct his team to ask and find answers to dozens of questions: Why is this building made of brick? Why does it face east? Why is it still standing?

Architect Jane Loefgren, who worked with Childress' firm for five years in the early 1980s before joining him at DU, found that every day with Childress provided a tutorial in a different subject. On one residential project in the Colorado mountains, she recalled, the plans incorporated fieldstone from the site. To ensure that the stone retain its natural character, Childress asked Loefgren to learn everything about its properties and condition. That meant working with a scientist, who instructed Loefgren in the care and feeding of lichen—essential knowledge for preserving the fieldstone's color and texture.

Stories like that ring familiar to Prosser. "Cab's passion to get things right was so intense that he perhaps went beyond most of his peers, which I think is really quite special," he said.

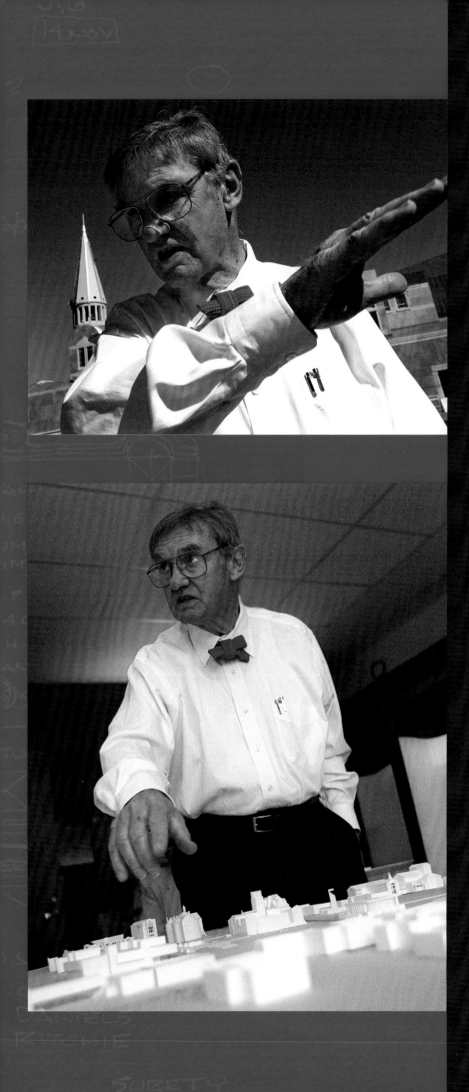

In 1990, casting about for a substantial project to keep his firm afloat and to finish his career, Childress wrote two unsolicited letters—one to the chief executive of Copper Mountain Resort and one to the DU chancellor, Dan Ritchie. Years earlier, Childress had enjoyed a rewarding working relationship with Ritchie, designing the headquarters building for his ranch property in the mountains. They had also collaborated on a remote retreat, Granny's Castle, located near a mountain feature known as Granny's Nipple and a lacy ridge called Granny's Nightcap.

As Childress recounted it, the letters began with an earnest offer to put his talents at their disposal: "Gentlemen, you have two well-started things that haven't been fouled up to this point, nothing that cannot be fixed. If you'll give me those, I'll give you the rest of my life."

Childress never heard from Copper Mountain Resort, but two years later, at the age of 60, he began his long, fruitful, and occasionally tempestuous association with DU. He served as university architect until his retirement in 1999, but continued to advise the design team as architect emeritus until his death.

Childress was hired, Mark Rodgers recalled, because he was honest, tenacious, and willing to speak his mind—qualities that appealed to Ritchie. "I think Dan loved that about Cab," Rodgers, the current university architect, said. "However, Dan also knew hiring him was a great risk, because at some point they were going to have their disagreements, which they did."

The scope of the DU project appealed to Childress' appetite for challenge. The campus presented a diverse array of architectural styles and represented a wide range of philosophical approaches to education. One of Childress' first goals was to build on the existing framework to make the campus an identifiable place.

"As a university architect," he told *Colorado Construction* magazine in 2002, "you have to start with the notion that a campus is not just a series of buildings. It's more like a village, a place where everything and everyone is connected."

Working on the campus, Childress drew upon all his life experiences—his hundreds of projects, his travels, his family life, his collection of images—to connect one end of campus with the other and to make each stop on the journey its own reward. He would pore over his carefully constructed collages—artistic assemblies of stairs, walls, towers, and columns—and then turn to his team to ask, "Do we have a window on campus this nice? A door this nice? If not, why not?"

That was, by no means, a license to copy. Instead, it was an invitation to excel. "Learn well," Childress once said, distilling his philosophy into a rhythmic mantra: "Learn well, learn well."

Learning can happen anywhere, but the learning process is exponentially more powerful when its backdrop has been designed to stimulate creativity, curiosity, and connections. Reflecting the influence of Colorado architect G. Cabell Childress, each University of Denver building constructed since the early 1990s has been crafted to foster the life of the mind. In classroom buildings and residence halls, students are invited to question, explore, collaborate, and dream. Nowhere is that more true than in F.W. Olin Hall, the Daniels College of Business building, and the King Lee and Shirley Nelson Residence Hall.

BUILDINGS FOR LIVING AND LEARNING

3

"An architect needs the skin of a rhinoceros and the finesse of a butterfly. You have to be tough and oh so gentle."

— G. CABELL CHILDRESS

THE UNIVERSITY'S NEW ACADEMIC AND RESIDENCE BUILDINGS ARE DESIGNED TO MAXIMIZE THE OPPORTUNITIES FOR LEARNING AND GROWTH. IN THE MARCUS COMMONS, PICTURED ON PAGE 44, DANIELS COLLEGE OF BUSINESS STUDENTS CAN GATHER FOR STUDY SESSIONS BETWEEN CLASSES. THE ROTUNDA IN OLIN HALL, SHOWN AT THE TOP OF THIS PAGE, PROVIDES INVITING SPACES FOR COLLABORATION. IN NELSON HALL, PICTURED AT THE BOTTOM OF THIS PAGE, THE ROOMS PROVIDE A COMFORTABLE HOME AWAY FROM HOME.

F.W. OLIN HALL SETS THE STANDARD

By the 1990s, the university's crumbling science facilities were beginning to take a toll on the program, hampering efforts to recruit top faculty and students. If Old Science Hall—with its leaky roof and bat colonies—served as a metaphor for the programs within, the message to prospective professors and students was counterproductive: This program awaits demolition.

F.W. OLIN HALL

F.W. Olin Hall

ARCHITECT OF RECORD
Davis Partnership Architects

CONTRACTOR
Gerald H. Phipps

BUDGET
$7.8 million

SQUARE FOOTAGE
40,000

Clearly, a different message needed to be conveyed. To that end, F.W. Olin Hall became the first new undergraduate building to rise on campus in nearly thirty years. Olin was built to give the sciences a worthy home and, in part, to communicate the university's attitude toward academics. Its copper-roofed dome and its bright yellow rotunda testified to the grandeur of inquiry and to sky-high aspirations.

Before Olin Hall's welcome debut, undergraduate biology, chemistry, and physics students had to traverse the south side of campus for classes taught in an assortment of aging structures surrounded by dirt parking lots. In addition to Old Science Hall, a relic dating back to 1911, the buildings included Knudson Hall, John Greene Hall, and the Boettcher Center. In the words of today's chancellor, Robert D. Coombe, then chairman of the chemistry department and later dean of the Division of Natural Sciences, Mathematics, and Engineering, "It was like the frontier down there."

TRAVEL
FOR INSIGHT AND INSPIRATION

A self-described and proud regionalist, Cab Childress believed that to understand any given project site, you needed to travel 100 miles to the north, south, east, and west. He also believed in borrowing good ideas from far-flung locales and the pages of history books.

As part of his preliminary research for university building projects, Childress assembled teams to travel together to other cities and countries to absorb best practices and ideas. For example, when contemplating the structure and character of Nelson Hall, DU's first residence hall in more than forty years, Childress and Rodgers decided they wanted to learn about how other institutions approached the concept of community living. With that in mind, they journeyed to Oxford and Cambridge to immerse themselves in the celebrated English model of housing and educating students. They were joined by Roscoe Hill, dean emeritus of the Divisions of Arts, Humanities, and Social Sciences, as well as Sheila Phelan Wright, then vice provost for undergraduate studies, and Todd Olson, formerly associate vice provost for campus life.

Childress was a proponent of traveling in numbers, the better to enhance his own understanding of the project's challenges. As Rodgers recalled, group excursions allowed the architects to see from different perspectives. They learned to look at a space with an educator's eyes, to see how it served academic goals as well as aesthetic priorities. The trips also created shared memories that could be drawn on as the design progressed. Finally, the experience served to remind the design team about the value of listening to one another and to the client.

At Oxford's Magdalen College, they learned that students preferred the 400-year-old halls to the newest residence facilities, despite the latter's modern conveniences. They learned that students can tell the difference between a structure built to last and one built to suffice. Just as important, they learned that students want to tap into a university's traditions, to feel part of a historical continuum.

IN DESIGNING OLIN HALL, CHILDRESS SOUGHT TO CREATE A BUILDING THAT COMPLEMENTED ITS NEIGHBORS WHILE OFFERING SCIENCE STUDENTS AN INSPIRATIONAL SETTING FOR THEIR WORK. THE BUILDING'S COPPER-TOPPED ELLIPTICAL DOME PRESENTED NUMEROUS LOGISTICAL CHALLENGES FOR THE CONSTRUCTION TEAM.

While the existing facilities were functional, they were far from optimal. Among other things, the learning spaces were small, antiquated, and inhospitable to advanced technology — a severe handicap for any reputable science program.

Remedying this situation meant raising a considerable sum. Given the business community's skepticism about the university's finances and future, that was no easy task, but then-Chancellor Dan Ritchie and the board of trustees put the university's fundraising campaign into overdrive. Robert M. Dores, chairman of DU's biology department, considered their efforts a boon to spirits as well as to the building budget.

"When Dan came on board, he was like a lightening rod. He exuded this 'can-do' mentality, and that was really the key. He simply electrified things," Dores said.

The first step was to secure funding from the prestigious F.W. Olin Foundation, known for promoting innovation in higher education. The foundation required the university to meet a host of benchmarks before rewarding it the project's $7.8 million cost. According to Mark Rodgers, current university architect, "One of the most important elements of this whole funding process was the fact that the Olin grant signified that the university was worth investing in."

A CATHEDRAL TO SCIENCE

F.W. Olin Hall was the first DU building designed by the Childress and Rodgers team. Knowing that this project would set the standard for all the construction to come, they approached their work with a heightened sense of its importance. Perhaps their biggest challenge was to integrate the new building into its setting, to establish its ties to the rest of the campus, and to make it seem both rooted and poised for the future.

Working with Hugh Brown, AIA, of Davis Partnership Architects, Childress and Rodgers formalized a conceptual design that nestled the new two-story building into a site flanked by campus outbuildings, mid-century apartment houses, and the imposing Boettcher Center. To identify the building as a DU property, the design for Olin nodded to the mix of materials and styles found in the precast concrete buildings to the west and north, and to the brick and trim Mary Reed Building on the other side of Iliff Avenue. In particular, Olin's exterior brick, granite, and limestone trim were meant to honor the Collegiate Gothic architecture of the Mary Reed Building and Margery Reed Hall.

F.W. OLIN HALL

2190 EAST ILIFF AVENUE

THE SECOND STORY OF THE OLIN HALL ROTUNDA OFFERS
SECLUDED SPOTS TO STUDY, WHILE THE GROUND FLOOR
PROVIDES AMPLE SPACE FOR GROUP GATHERINGS. AT
RIGHT, A LIMESTONE LIZARD, LOCATED ON OLIN HALL'S
BACK STAIRCASE, BORROWS FROM A MEDIEVAL TRADITION
OF INCORPORATING A REPRESENTATION OF A CHURCH
MOUSE IN ECCLESIASTICAL ARCHITECTURE. THE TRADITION
WAS UPDATED AT OLIN TO DEPICT A REPTILE COMMONLY
USED IN SCIENTIFIC RESEARCH.

By establishing a solid link to these university landmarks, Olin Hall's design helped connect the science program to the rest of campus.

In communicating the importance of the new academic building to the university landscape, Childress wanted to whisper rather than shout. With that in mind, he was careful to scale Olin Hall modestly. Rather than compete with its cohorts for attention, the building was intended to join the chorus. One of Childress' biggest challenges was ensuring that Olin Hall's architectural details complemented the visual grid defined by the nearby Boettcher Center and Cherrington Hall. Both Boettcher and Cherrington feature numerous precast columns that create a tightly spaced vertical pattern. To avoid clashing with those columns, Childress needed to ensure that Olin Hall's architectural elements were mathematically harmonious. Hence, the rounded windows in the rotunda are broken by carefully spaced supports that align with, but do not repeat, the patterns established with the Boettcher Center and Cherrington Hall. For Childress, working within the visual grid was necessary to subdue the existing chaos.

One of the hallmarks of the 40,000-square-foot Olin Hall is its copper-topped, cathedral-like elliptical dome, which shelters the light-infused rotunda. Until tackling Olin Hall, the building's general contractor, Gerald H. Phipps, had never fabricated a dome of this complexity. Despite misgivings from the builders, Childress was undeterred—a classic example of the architect's characteristic insistence on pushing craftsmanship to the next level. If the scientists at work in the building would be blazing new trails, so should the building's creators.

Located on the north side of the building, the rotunda serves as a contemplative spot for science students. The skylight, which is framed by a star-shaped, origami-style folded drywall plate, invites students to ponder the cosmos and reflect on the unknown. The rotunda also features curved windows that offer an expansive view of the campus, allowing students to step away from the microscopic view and enjoy the big picture. "Being in Olin is a little bit like being in a snow globe," Childress once said.

In early bids on the building, contractors consistently relegated the curved glass of the rotunda to "alternate" status because of its expense. Determined to see the design executed according to its original specifications, Ritchie asked the Olin Foundation to cover the $70,000 shortfall for the customized glass. Later, after seeing the rotunda in use, Childress labeled the choice to respect the original design as a "tiny, tiny decision that made all the difference."

Besides housing the biology and chemistry departments, Olin Hall features two ninety-five-seat lecture halls, eleven fully equipped science laboratories, a demonstration computer lab, and two seminar rooms. The "owners" of the building—Coombe, Dores, and the science faculty—worked closely with Childress and Rodgers to create roomy teaching and learning facilities, large storage compartments for biology and chemistry equipment, and expansive lab space.

Initially, the building's owners thought of their new structure in terms of needs—everything from new technology to flexible teaching spaces and comfortable lecture halls. But, Dores noted, Childress challenged them to think as well of the building's overall feel. "When I told him we wanted better lab chairs, he said, 'No, no, no. You have to think bigger than that. Tell me what's most important to you.' Cab was less worried about whether our science tables were black or checkered and more concerned with the mood and atmosphere we wanted to create. I remember him saying, 'What do you want people to see first when they walk in Olin, and how will that help your mission?'"

Thanks to this process, Coombe said, Olin is not simply a collection of offices and labs. Instead, it offers a variety of cheerful and intimate learning spaces that foster collaboration among students and professors. "Olin's success has to do with the interaction between faculty and students on a personal level that certainly goes beyond the normal classroom environment," Coombe explained. "It gets to the question of how you build structures that promote intellectual engagement, the type of spaces that foster that sort of communication, as well as the sort of spaces that are best for promoting the creation of ideas."

WITH ITS COMPACT SPACES AND JUDICIOUS USE OF SQUARE FOOTAGE, OLIN HALL WAS INFLUENCED BY CHILDRESS' SERVICE IN THE NAVY. HIS TIME ON SHIPS GAVE HIM AN APPRECIATION FOR INNOVATIVE STORAGE SOLUTIONS AND FLEXIBLE SPACES THAT COULD BE RECONFIGURED FOR MULTIPLE USES.

OLIN HALL ACCOMMODATES THE SCIENCE FACULTY'S EMPHASIS ON CLOSE COLLABORATION WITH STUDENTS. IN LABS AND OFFICES, IN CLASSROOMS AND IN STUDY AREAS, STUDENTS FIND AN ENVIRONMENT CONDUCIVE TO EXCHANGING IDEAS AND ASKING QUESTIONS.

A BUILDING TO ATTRACT THE BEST AND BRIGHTEST

Like Olin Hall, the Daniels College of Business was designed to offer students a learning experience characterized by interaction with faculty and peers. It was also designed to tell students that their work matters, that their future is worth a sizable investment.

DANIELS COLLEGE

Daniels College of Business

ARCHITECT OF RECORD
Anderson Mason Dale Architects

CONTRACTOR
Adolfson & Peterson, Inc.

BUDGET
$25 million

SQUARE FOOTAGE
110,000

Housing the university's internationally renowned business program, the Daniels College of Business is positioned at the gateway to campus, on the southwest corner of University Boulevard and Evans Avenue. When the $25 million building opened in 1999, it was one of the university's largest academic buildings, with 110,000 square feet of classroom, office, and common space. Its cutting-edge technology and flexible classrooms testified to the university's focus on innovation and on preparation for forthcoming challenges. Its solid, enduring materials spoke to the Daniels College of Business' core values, its emphasis on ethics and integrity.

"I've always thought of buildings as metaphors for quality, as well as instruments for contextual and cultural change. In the Daniels building, we have a state-of-the-art building and an environment that attracts the best and brightest students and professors," said Jim Griesemer, who was dean of the college when the new building first welcomed students.

The driving force behind the transformation of the business school was the late Bill Daniels, known to Coloradans as a cable television pioneer and as a visionary philanthropist. His goal was to create a business school that stressed ethics and values, while also preparing students to become better business and community leaders. In 1989, with that goal in mind, Daniels provided the university with an $11 million challenge grant. The challenge was met just five years later, making Daniels' contribution worth a total of $22 million. Said Daniels at the time, "If these facilities help create a new generation of business leaders around the world, my financial support will prove to be a great investment."

For Childress, one of the biggest challenges associated with executing Daniels' vision grew out of the site. The land allocated for the new building fell between two long-standing structures with strong, even outspoken architectural characteristics: the Collegiate Gothic design and diminutive stature of Margery Reed Hall, built in 1928, and the massive bulk of University Hall. The challenge was made more complicated by Daniels' request that the business school be housed in two wings, one for faculty and one for students and classrooms.

Working with DU architectural consultant Margie Soo Hoo Lee, and Ron Mason and Andy Nielsen of Anderson Mason Dale Architects, Childress aimed to pay respect to both of the new building's neighbors. His choice of materials —the exterior features more than 500,000 specially made "DU blend" red bricks—ties the building to Margery Reed Hall. With its limestone trim and steel windows, the Daniels College also mimics Margery Reed's ornamentation and fenestration. The three-story classroom wing of the building slopes toward the two-story Margery Reed Hall and repeats its modest scale.

The six-story office wing, featuring the Daniels College's main entrance, sits on the south side of the building near University Hall. To marry the new building to the old, Childress gave the Daniels College a roofline that followed the pitch and angles of University Hall. As with Olin Hall, Childress was determined to integrate the building into its setting and thus show that the business program was part of a larger whole.

For the inside of the building, Childress and team chose to create warmth by incorporating cast-in-place concrete

floors, Appalachian rift-sawn white oak trim, and Welsh quarry floor tiles. The building shelters twenty-one tiered and seminar-style classrooms, fifteen meeting rooms, 132 faculty and staff offices, a business resource center, a computer and software center, a commons area, and a boardroom for trustee and community business meetings. All the rooms benefit from technologically advanced infrastructure, which means students can launch their laptops in the Marcus Commons, while professors can share video and audio materials in classrooms and offices.

Classroom designs were inspired by a format used at the University of Virginia's Darden School of Business, famous for its "case method" approach to business education. The case method immerses students in real-life situations. It also challenges them to master all the particulars of a case study.

Implementing case methodology requires that professors interact directly and intensely with students. To stimulate interpersonal dynamics, Childress created "case rooms" that depart from the typical lecture hall format and instead sport a wide center aisle. This allows the professor to leave the "bullpen" area at the focal point of the room and walk

EXPANSIVE WINDOWS ENCOURAGE STUDENTS FROM
ALL MAJORS AND DISCIPLINES TO MAKE USE OF
THE MARCUS COMMONS. THE ROOM IS GENERALLY
FILLED WITH STUDENTS FROM EARLY MORNING
UNTIL EVENING.

into the seating area, where it is easy to talk directly to each student. This way, no student can hide in the back of the room; no one can escape participation.

The center aisle also promotes interaction by requiring that every student gaze toward the middle of the room. That way, they are likelier to make eye contact with their professor and fellow students. To facilitate this eye contact, the architects relied on a specifically calculated distance from the left side of the horseshoe-shaped room to the right side. When Griesemer traveled to the Darden School to study its case-based classroom designs, he learned from one of the professors that this type of design, by facilitating eye contact, fosters discussion among students, as well as with the professor. "He said to me, 'If you can't see my eyes, you can't talk to me.' Our case rooms at DU were specifically sized by seeing the eyes," Griesemer recalled.

The classroom-generated discussions can continue in the roomy Marcus Commons, considered the heart and soul of the Daniels College building. With its various seating and dining arrangements, the room invites students to collaborate on group projects or share a cup of coffee with friends. Initially, Griesemer worried that too much square footage and money were being channeled into this meeting/eating facility, but his fears were dispelled on the third day that Marcus Commons was open to students. The room was filled to capacity.

The Marcus Commons' doors open to the west, to Graduation Green and the rest of the campus. This positioning encourages nonbusiness students and other members of the university community to take advantage of the relaxing environment. Rodgers believes that this creates a sense of inclusiveness. "It all goes back to what the university is and why we did what we did here," he said. "We're trying to drive interactions and create comfortable places where you don't have to worry about what you're wearing."

CONFERENCE ROOMS, OFFICES, AND STUDY AREAS ALL ADHERE TO TWENTY-FIRST CENTURY IDEAS ABOUT EDUCATION: STUDENTS NEED OPPORTUNITIES TO WORK IN TEAMS, INTERACT WITH PROFESSORS, AND EXCHANGE IDEAS WITH PEERS. THEY ALSO NEED TIME FOR QUIET REFLECTION.

IN THE MARSICO INVESTMENT CENTER, PICTURED AT BOTTOM RIGHT, STUDENTS LEARN HOW TO MANAGE AN INVESTMENT PORTFOLIO. THE CENTER WAS MADE POSSIBLE BY A GIFT FROM DU ALUMNI TOM AND CYDNEY MARSICO.

NELSON HALL SETS THE STAGE FOR MEMORIES

Mark Rodgers carries around a handful of baby pictures in his wallet. Several of the images feature his three children. One showcases Nelson Hall.

"Nelson Hall was my baby because it was the first project where I was the pilot," Rodgers said. His task in designing the residence hall, affectionately known as "the castle," was to create a backdrop for memorable experiences, the kind of memories that build long-term affection for the institution.

N E L S O N   H A L L

King Lee and Shirley Nelson Residence Hall

ARCHITECT OF RECORD
Bennett Wagner & Grody Architects, PC

CONTRACTOR
Haselden Construction

BUDGET
$40 million

SQUARE FOOTAGE
155,000

Named after DU alumni King Lee and Shirley Nelson, who helped fund the building, the five-story Nelson Hall opened to sophomores, juniors, and seniors in August 2002. It was the first residence building constructed on campus in forty years.

When the Nelsons made their gift to the university, they asked for a building that would make a difference in the academic development of its residents. That was just the kind of challenge that suited Rodgers' appetite for conceptual design. Heeding Childress' advice to "respect what's been done through the ages," Rodgers began his task by studying the full range of structures created to house large numbers of people — everything from barracks and dormitories to hotels and resorts.

The primary model for Nelson Hall grew out of a research trip to England made by Rodgers, Childress, and several faculty and staff members. They visited eleven different colleges in Cambridge and Oxford, assessing the living arrangements at each. What became immediately apparent was that students there consistently preferred the 300- to 400-year-old stone residences to the facilities built within the last thirty years. That's because the older buildings offered a variety of living arrangements—suites, singles, doubles, and even triples. Additionally, Rodgers said, the students appreciated the central courtyards and staircases that provide opportunities to interact.

The $40 million Nelson Hall borrows from all the good ideas that Rodgers and his collaborators collected. Unlike traditional "dormitory" environments, where students are essentially warehoused, Nelson Hall mimics the best hotels in the ways that it welcomes a diverse cross-section of individuals. It draws from English colleges in the ways that it encourages faculty-student interaction. Finally, the building calls upon the hospitality industry and a long tradition of communal architecture to offer multiple settings for socializing and networking.

With its 155,000 square feet of living space and its underground parking garage, Nelson Hall provides a wide array of room plans—including standard singles, doubles, and triples, as well as suites, apartments, and common areas. The options acknowledge the individual tastes and preferences of every student. Some accommodations have terrific views and small floor plans, while others offer larger floor plans with less dramatic views. A couple of floors are dedicated to the university's living and learning communities, which bring together students with a common passion or interest. In addition to sharing a dedicated floor in a residence hall, participants in living and learning communities get together for seminars and programs that focus on the community's theme.

Located on the west side of campus, Nelson Hall uses the university's thematic palette of red brick and limestone trim under a standing-seam copper roof. The building's five-ton, copper-clad tower tells residents that they are living someplace out of the ordinary. Topped by a thirty-foot spire and a gold-leafed finial, the 123-foot tower gives the building its castle-like feeling. The tower also breaks up the mass of the building and engages passersby.

MUCH OF THE DESIGN IN NELSON HALL MAKES REFERENCE TO THE MARY REED BUILDING. ITS ARCHES, FIXTURES, WINDOWS, AND TOWER LINK IT TO BELOVED TRADITIONS IN CAMPUS ARCHITECTURE.

NELSON HALL ANCHORS THE SOUTHWEST SIDE OF CAMPUS
AND OFFERS BOTH MOUNTAIN AND DOWNTOWN VIEWS
TO ITS STUDENT RESIDENTS. ITS DISTINCTIVE TOWER
SERVES AS A WAY-FINDING BEACON FOR STUDENTS
HEADED TO THE BUILDING FROM ACROSS CAMPUS.

STUDENTS MAKE MAXIMUM
USE OF NELSON HALL'S
MANY SPACES FOR PLAYING,
STUDYING, AND ENJOYING
THE COMPANY OF FRIENDS.

NELSON HALL OFFERS A VARIETY
OF ROOM CONFIGURATIONS
AND STYLES TO ACCOMMODATE
THE DIFFERENT PREFERENCES
OF STUDENT RESIDENTS.

In addition to accommodating 435 students, Nelson Hall provides two apartments for faculty members. This idea was lifted from Cambridge and Oxford, where the dons traditionally have kept rooms, the better to mentor the young adults in their orbit. The faculty apartment in Nelson Hall provides gracious accommodations for visiting professors or new faculty members who have yet to find quarters off campus. Ideally, they will join students in the dining hall or even invite them to participate in a book club or study session.

Nelson Hall also offers a large sun deck and a spacious English-style dining hall, open to all members of the university community. Like the bedrooms themselves, the dining hall was designed to cater to individual preferences. Depending on their mood, students can choose from small, secluded tables for private meals over an open book or large tables for dining with friends.

Reminiscent of many English colleges, Nelson also features a courtyard with lush grass. Accessed by staircases that descend from all four sides on the building's interior, the courtyard gives residents a place to gather in groups or to study in solitude. It also brings sunlight and warmth into the dining hall and various lounge areas.

For Rodgers, the dining hall, courtyard, and common areas are opportune backdrops for kindling lifelong friendships and making memories. But just as important are the staircases, which people ascend and descend on a predictable schedule — going to class, coming from dinner. Pass someone on the staircase at a certain time each day, Rodgers explained, and you eventually strike up an acquaintance. "That's where you meet that cute girl from international studies, that teaching assistant from accounting, the hockey player."

And the rest becomes history.

NELSON HALL BOASTS AN "OXFORDIAN" DINING
HALL, WHERE STUDENTS CAN SHARE MEALS—AND
IDEAS—WITH PROFESSORS.

A CROSSROADS FOR THE CAMPUS COMMUNITY

Just three years after Nelson Hall debuted, Rodgers began design on a five-story, 369-bed residence hall that, when it opened in fall 2008, set a new standard for residence life at DU. While working on Nagel Hall, made possible by a generous donation from DU trustee Ralph Nagel and his wife, Trish, Rodgers used Nelson Hall as his primer. It provided textbook instruction on what to do and what to do better.

What to do better meant advancing what current Chancellor Robert Coombe calls "a bubbling, percolating intellectual culture on campus." In addition to spaces

NAGEL HALL

Nagel Hall

ARCHITECT OF RECORD
H+L Architecture

CONTRACTOR
Gerald H. Phipps Inc.

BUDGET
$40 million

SQUARE FOOTAGE
155,000

that encourage student interaction and collaborative work, the building features a studio for painting and sculpture. The garden level incorporates faculty offices and research spaces for the psychology department. Just steps away from the main dining and social areas, an experimental classroom will allow the university's Center for Teaching and Learning to test new ideas about effective instruction.

Situated north of Nelson Hall, the building's exterior features a copper-topped tower that links it to other new buildings and that marks it against the university's skyline. Inside, the first three floors house sophomores, while the remaining floors have apartments for juniors and seniors. In response to student requests, Nagel Hall also offers a food court on the ground floor.

"A critical role for a university architect is continuing to complement what the institution has built without duplication," Rodgers said. "The design of Nelson Hall celebrates its placement as a destination through such notable aspects as its 'Oxfordian' dining hall and its cloistered courtyard. Nagel Hall is meant to be a contrasting crossroads where its open 'front yard' and frenetic dining area invite the entire academic community to interact throughout the day and night."

All too often, the metaphor used to discuss the modern-day university incorporates an ivory tower. That image suggests a disconnect, a haughty remove from the everyday concerns of the community. At the University of Denver, the architecture retires the ivory tower in favor of elements that beckon and welcome the community. The stone and copper Ritchie Center invites Coloradans to partake of campus amenities, while the spacious theaters at the Newman Center seek to share artistic bounty with people from all walks of life. And at the Chambers Center, the university opens its doors to community organizations that work to better the lives of Colorado's women and girls.

BUILDINGS THAT WELCOME THE COMMUNITY

4

"Place is many things.
It's the landscape, the culture.
It's the sun, it's the moon."

— DAN RITCHIE

ARTS PATRONS FROM ALL OVER THE DENVER METROPOLITAN AREA ASSEMBLE IN THE JUNE SWANER GATES CONCERT HALL, PICTURED AT FAR LEFT, FOR AN EVENING OF ENTERTAINMENT. AT THE CHAMBERS CENTER FOR THE ADVANCEMENT OF WOMEN, COLORADO WOMEN'S ORGANIZATIONS AND STUDENTS FROM THE WOMEN'S COLLEGE HAVE ACCESS TO THE BUILDING'S SPACIOUS GARDEN ROOM, SHOWN AT TOP. MEANWHILE, COMMENCEMENT AUDIENCES GATHER OUTSIDE THE RITCHIE CENTER TO CONTEMPLATE THE FUTURE FACING NEW GRADUATES.

A SPORTS AND RECREATION CENTER FOR THE CAMPUS AND COMMUNITY

In fall 1999, the Daniel L. Ritchie Center for Sports & Wellness opened to the DU and Denver communities. With its recreation center, natatorium, ice rink, gymnasium, and hockey and basketball arena, the venue was designed to foster a campus culture that nurtures mind, body, and spirit, while providing the Denver community a much-needed resource.

RITCHIE CENTER

Daniel L. Ritchie Center for Sports & Wellness

ARCHITECT OF RECORD
Davis Partnership Architects

CONTRACTOR
Calcon Constructors

BUDGET
$74 million

SQUARE FOOTAGE
440,000

The building's importance to its on- and off-campus constituencies is represented by its crowning jewel: the gold-leaf Carl M. Williams bell tower, made possible by a gift from Williams himself, a DU honorary life trustee. At 192 feet, the tower can be seen for miles: It has become a Denver landmark, not just a university building.

Before the Ritchie Center's development, DU's athletic facilities were represented by the Alumni Gymnasium, a dilapidated structure built in 1910, as well as a 1940s-era surplus blimp hangar, which served as home for the Pioneer hockey team. Both structures testified to decades of benign neglect. Neither seemed, in their deteriorating state, an inspiring site for peak performances or conference championships. Replacing them was a top priority, and eventually both would be demolished, the blimp hangar by implosion, to make way for a facility that could host an NCAA Division I athletics program.

CHILDRESS' MANY SKETCHES OF THE
RITCHIE CENTER SHOW HOW HE WORKED TO
VARY THE ROOFLINES AND ADD VISUAL
INTEREST TO THE BUILDING'S HORIZONTAL
FORM. BELOW, AN EARLY ILLUSTRATION
OF THE RITCHIE CENTER INCLUDES AN
ORANGERIE TO THE SOUTH END OF THE
STRUCTURE. THE ORANGERIE WAS LATER
ELIMINATED FROM THE PLANS BECAUSE OF
BUDGET CONSTRAINTS. ON PAGE 81, THE
WILLIAMS TOWER TAKES SHAPE. CHILDRESS
COUNTED THIS VIEW OF THE EMERGING
TOWER AS ONE OF HIS FAVORITES. IT
REPRESENTED THE CLOSEST IT WOULD COME,
IN HIS LIFETIME, TO A RUIN.

A DREAM RESURRECTED

In the early 1990s, Davis Partnership Architects had been commissioned to develop plans for an all-encompassing athletics facility. Architect Hugh Brown, as well as former DU athletic director Jack MacDonald and facilities director Jerry Schilling, visited numerous collegiate facilities around the country before proceeding with an ambitious schematic design. The estimated cost for the building ranged from $50 million to $60 million, a sum far beyond the $17 million originally envisioned by the trustees. As a result, plans for the new building were temporarily shelved.

When the time came to rekindle plans for a state-of-the-art athletics facility, Dan Ritchie revisited the original drawings. "It was lovely," Ritchie said of the first design, "but it could have been in Winnipeg or Miami." He was adamant that the building should represent its Colorado and Denver location. After all, the university is a Denver institution; it belongs to and serves the city.

For Ritchie, the best architecture tells a story about the place it calls home—it roots visitors in a specific spot on the map. "When I think of this part of the world, I think of

stone," Ritchie said. Just as important, he added, he thinks of culture. The culture of the West is less cloistered than that of the East; it's more open, friendlier. Its attitude toward the elements and the spiritual draws from a confluence of cultures. To illustrate his point, Ritchie recounted a story about the West's native tribes. Before the arrival of Europeans, tribal artisans made exquisite rugs that were, however beautiful, never symmetrical, never perfect. "They didn't want to make the great spirit mad. And that attitude toward perfection is a characteristic of the West," he explained.

In 1992, Ritchie hired Cab Childress to modify Davis Partnership's original design. A year later, he convinced the board of trustees to move ahead with the project, and then began contacting potential donors. He also put $15 million of his own money into the project, believing that the facility would communicate the university's bold ambitions to all who encountered it.

By this time, the scope of the project had increased from 290,000 square feet to 440,000 square feet to accommodate such additions as the Joy Burns Arena. The final costs of the project had increased as well, growing to $74 million. For Childress and Rodgers, the pressure was on to spend the money wisely and create a building that would redefine the university's relationship with the community.

Childress chose his materials carefully, selecting for his palette three that would interact vibrantly with the Colorado sun—sandstone, Indiana limestone, and copper. The sandstone—which Childress described as "nothing more than sunshine that has been congealed"—came from one small quarry in Utah. Ritchie was delighted with the choice—its personality coincided with his concept of a Western material. "The stone is not uniform," he noted. Rather, every slab differs in texture and pattern. That made it the perfect material for Childress' unadorned design. Like a rustic pine dining table or a stone fireplace, the building expresses a Western aesthetic that prefers simple, unvarnished forms.

Because the project called for huge quantities, the university bought the sandstone in advance of construction to give the quarry adequate time to fill the order. The sandstone was delivered in large blocks, so for the customized installations, the university hired masons, notably Chuck Nacos of Fort Collins-based Soderberg Masonry, to chisel the stone, some of it on site. "I call the Ritchie Center Chuck's cathedral," Childress once remarked, noting that the craftsmanship in the stonework reminded him of European masterpieces. For his part, Nacos appreciated Childress' insistence on building to last. "One important thing I

learned from Cab was that to get these great buildings, you had to have the right owner, who insists on doing things right and building for the long term. For Cab, we would rise to any occasion. We would go out of our way to help him."

Childress also looked to European models when it came time to design the Williams Tower, which was added to the plans sometime after the initial drawings for the building had been drafted. "Dan called me on a Friday night and said, 'Let's put a tower on the wellness center,'" Childress recalled. Ritchie's reasoning? He wanted a tower that could be illuminated when the Pioneers won a hockey game. It would report the good news to the entire city.

Intrigued, Childress began reviewing hundreds of buildings with famous towers, studying their relationship to the host building, their proportion and scale. Then he tried to imagine the buildings without their towers. And that, he explained, was when he came to realize that towers signify aspiration, that they speak to the best qualities of a university and a city. Later, he asked Ritchie about his favorite tower, and among the many possible choices, Ritchie singled out the towers on the Cathedral of Our Lady of Chartres. Ritchie was particularly taken with the cathedral's south tower, the older of the two towers and, to his mind, the simpler. Sometime after the completion of the Williams Tower, Childress made a pilgrimage to France to see the Gothic icon for himself.

Inside the Ritchie Center, Childress and his office worked side by side with the architects from the Davis Partnership to create facilities that added to, rather than competed with, other venues and buildings in Denver. For instance, unlike other Denver-area sports venues, which seem to be configured with ticket-taking and crowd control foremost in mind, the Ritchie Center encourages event

CHILDRESS DELIBERATELY LEFT THE WALLS INSIDE THE WILLIAMS TOWER UNADORNED, BELIEVING THAT LATER OCCUPANTS SHOULD MAKE THEIR OWN MARK AND THAT "THE QUICKEST WAY TO KILL SOMETHING IS TO COMPLETE IT." HONORARY LIFE TRUSTEE CARL WILLIAMS AND TRUSTEE SCOTT REIMAN EVENTUALLY COMMISSIONED A MURAL FOR THE SPACE. THE BARTON LACROSSE STADIUM, AT RIGHT, IS THE ONLY COLLEGE STADIUM IN THE UNITED STATES BUILT SOLELY FOR LACROSSE.

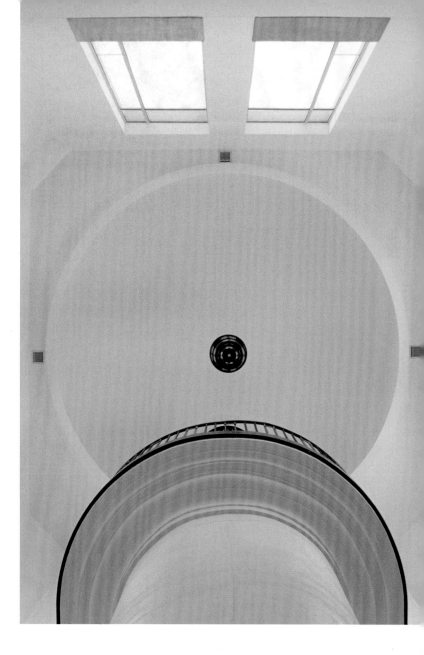

CARILLON

Once upon a time in the Old World, tower bells tolled a warning or signaled the start of a market day or a holiday. In their University of Denver incarnation, tower bells sound a festive note.

Periodically throughout the school year, the sixty-five-bell carillon in the Ritchie Center's Carl Williams Tower is summoned to life by DU carillonneur Todd Fair and by the Lamont School of Music's handful of carillon students. On the second Sunday of each December, the Denver community is invited to share in the riches when Fair presents a free holiday concert.

A carillon is made up of a specific number of bells—the minimum number is twenty-three, while a concert carillon has at least forty-eight. The smallest bell in DU's carillon is the size of a modest flower pot, while the largest is the size of a Volkswagen Beetle. These bells are mechanically activated via a keyboard and foot pedals. The instrument is tuned to produce a certain harmonic sound when specific bells are played together. Because of humidity and temperature variations, the bells must be tuned each year by adjusting the springs and the connecting rods to the clavier.

The university's concert carillon was cast in 1999 by the world-renowned Royal Eljsbouts Bellfoundry in the Netherlands. At the time of its debut, DU's carillon ranked as the world's tenth largest by total weight. Some carillon aficionados consider it the fourth best—a designation bestowed upon it because all the bells were cast at the same time. Many of the world's largest carillons have had bells added over time. Because the original tuning of each bell relative to all the others is done in the foundry, the addition of a bell after installation can result in flawed tuning.

attendees to wander the concourse and view other sporting events that may be going on simultaneously, perhaps a swim meet or a gymnastics competition. The goal, Mark Rodgers explained, was to expose visitors to other athletic activities, sports they might want to try themselves. "We designed the building with the idea of promoting wellness, thereby hopefully inspiring patrons to become physically active and enjoy and pursue fitness," Rodgers said.

The building's facilities include the Magness Arena for hockey, basketball, and concerts; the Gates Field House for indoor soccer, volleyball, and basketball; the Joy Burns Arena for ice skating and club hockey; the Hamilton Gymnasium for gymnastics and volleyball; the El Pomar Natatorium for swimming and diving; and the Coors Fitness Center for workouts and training. Outside, the Peter Barton Lacrosse Stadium and the Benjamin F. Stapleton Jr. Tennis Pavilion provide first-rate facilities for the Pioneer teams.

The $5 million Barton Lacrosse Stadium, which was dedicated in April 2005, is the only college stadium in the United States built solely for lacrosse. It was made possible by a gift from Laura Barton, who named the stadium in honor of her late husband, an entrepreneur, cable television executive, and adjunct professor at the Daniels College of Business. The 2,000-seat stadium features Hansen sandstone, limestone walls, and a seventy-five-foot tower topped by a copper-shingled spire. Besides hosting the Pioneer men's and women's lacrosse teams, the facility is also home to the Colorado Lacrosse Foundation.

The nearby Stapleton Tennis Pavilion, which was completed in 1998, provides practice and competition facilities for the men's and women's tennis teams. It features six outdoor courts and grandstand seating for 300, as well as locker rooms, a pro shop, concession stands, and coaches' offices. To complement the Ritchie Center, both pavilions utilize stone and copper.

During the academic year, the various indoor and outdoor venues are used by the Pioneer athletics teams and by DU students participating in club sports. They are also open to Coloradans who want to join an intramural team or work out on state-of-the-art equipment. When the academic year ends, the facilities host hundreds of school-age children who come to hone their skills at summer sports camps.

On any given evening, the athletics complex is used by young and old, novice and devotee, and on game days, fan and foe.

THE MARION GOTTESFELD ROOM, SHOWN AT LEFT AND NAMED AFTER A LONGTIME FRIEND OF THE UNIVERSITY, IS AVAILABLE FOR CONFERENCES, WEDDING RECEPTIONS, AND OTHER EVENTS. THE STAPLETON TENNIS PAVILION AND EL POMAR NATATORIUM, AS WELL AS THE VARIOUS ARENAS AND GYMNASIUMS, PROVIDE THE PIONEER SPORTS TEAMS WITH SPACE TO PRACTICE AND COMPETE. MEANWHILE, STUDENTS, FACULTY, AND FITNESS ENTHUSIASTS FROM THE COMMUNITY ENJOY WORKOUTS IN THE COORS FITNESS CENTER, TOP RIGHT.

THE FEISTY PIONEER HOCKEY TEAM ENJOYS HOME
ICE ADVANTAGE IN MAGNESS ARENA. THE TEAM
WON BACK-TO-BACK NATIONAL CHAMPIONSHIPS
IN 2004 AND 2005.

AN ARTS FACILITY TO ENHANCE DENVER'S CULTURAL TAPESTRY

Since its founding in 1924 by the late Florence Lamont Hinman, a renowned voice teacher, the Lamont School of Music had sought a facility to complement the talents of its faculty and staff. Despite a number of moves from inadequate building to inadequate building, the university's music program held its own, adding to

NEWMAN CENTER

Robert and Judi Newman Center for the Performing Arts

ARCHITECT OF RECORD
Anderson Mason Dale

CONTRACTOR
PCL Construction Services, Inc.

BUDGET
$67 million

SQUARE FOOTAGE
180,000

Denver's artistic community and training some of the country's top talent. "It was a pretty decent school of music," director Joe Docksey recalled, "however, we had no real dedicated facilities."

That changed with the 2002 debut of the Robert and Judi Newman Center for the Performing Arts, made possible by the generosity of trustee Robert Newman and his wife, both longtime arts patrons and university supporters. The 181,298-square-foot facility gave the Lamont School of Music a worthy setting for its next chapters. It also gave the city of Denver a host of distinctive venues — for sharing and showcasing the talents of DU students and faculty, for productions by local and traveling performance groups, and for programming that enhances Denver's cultural scene.

THE HAMILTON FAMILY RECITAL HALL, SHOWN ON PAGE 89, FEATURES A 2,500-PIPE ORGAN AND AN INTIMATE STAGE FOR RECITALS AND CHAMBER MUSIC.

CHILDRESS DREW ON A LIFETIME OF
PROJECTS WHEN HE CREATED THE
NEWMAN CENTER FOR THE PERFORMING
ARTS. FOR EXAMPLE, HIS WORK FOR THE
COLORADO SCHOOL FOR THE DEAF AND
THE BLIND TAUGHT HIM MUCH ABOUT
SOUND ENHANCEMENT, WHICH HELPED
HIM UNDERSTAND THE ACOUSTICS
CHALLENGES ASSOCIATED WITH
REHEARSAL AND PERFORMANCE SPACES.
THE MODEL AT RIGHT SHOWS THE
VARIOUS HALLS AND VENUES OPENING
TOWARD AN UNROOFED COURTYARD.
THAT PLAN WAS SCRAPPED IN FAVOR
OF PROVIDING AN INDOOR LOBBY THAT
COULD SERVE ALL THE THEATERS.

AT THE NEWMAN CENTER'S WEST ENTRANCE,
SHOWN ON PAGE 91, MUSIC AND THEATER
PATRONS GATHER BEFORE SHOWS AND DURING
INTERMISSIONS. THE BUILDING ENJOYS AN
ACTIVE NIGHTLIFE, WHEN STUDENTS AND
COMMUNITY MEMBERS COME TOGETHER TO
SAVOR THE PERFORMING ARTS.

For the Lamont School of Music, the new facilities provided a welcome respite from a past characterized by frequent relocations and imperfect accommodations. A decade after the school's 1941 merger with the University of Denver, it was utilizing Buchtel Chapel for rehearsals and concerts, while some of its faculty were housed on the fourth floor of the Mary Reed Building. Later, the school moved to a building known as the Green House at 2100 South Josephine Street before relocating to a former men's dormitory in 1978. Practice facilities were so unsatisfactory that the band and orchestra were relegated to rehearsing in Carnegie Library while holding performances in the auditorium of the General Classroom Building, now Sturm Hall. In 1985, still another move took the school to the Houston Fine Arts Center on the Park Hill campus in northeast Denver.

Three years later, Docksey was hired as the school's director. From the beginning, he dreamed of giving his 300 music students a top-of-the-line space for practicing their art form. His dreams were expedited when DU completed a deal to sell the Houston Fine Arts Center to the city of Denver. With proceeds from the sale of the center and the Park Hill campus on hand, Childress went to work envisioning the facility that would match Docksey's high expectations.

The first task was site selection. Childress initially wanted to tuck the facility into the campus. "I hide. I shelter," he once said, describing his urge to site buildings discreetly. But Ritchie was adamant that the building be easy to find, that drivers and pedestrians along University Boulevard see its marquee and understand that they were welcome to partake of the pleasures inside.

Working with Docksey, as well as Andy Nielsen and John Everin of Anderson Mason Dale, P.C., Childress, Rodgers, and other members of the DU architectural team spent many long hours at the drafting table. Childress' prior experience had prepared him well for the task at hand. Years earlier, he had designed the dance and theater building at the University of Colorado at Boulder. On his various travels, he had studied the acoustics of medieval churches. As longtime friend and fellow architect John Prosser noted, Childress' fascination with history, philosophy, and architecture were the best preparation for work on a performing arts complex. "When you analyze it, theater is the ultimate great expression of design," Prosser said.

This was a job that Childress relished, building a space for people who, as he put it, "understand what two o'clock in the morning is." In other words, life doesn't stop, and creativity doesn't cease, when the five o'clock whistle blows. "The artist lives around the clock," Childress explained.

To illustrate his point, Childress was fond of telling a story about his preliminary research for the building. On a visit to the Lamont School's Park Hill digs, he spied a violin on a table and admired its workmanship. Docksey told him that the violin was worth a million dollars, that a dedicated musician would save and save and even mortgage the house to buy such an instrument. For a year, the artist would tour with that violin and play it passionately. And then, in a plot twist worthy of an opera, the artist might lose the mortgaged house. And perhaps even the instrument. But for one magical year, the artist knew perfection.

That tale of creative abandon inspired Childress to strive for a building worthy of artistic passion. For ideas, he turned to the architecture of one of music's foremost cities, Vienna—a cultural capital he knew only from photographs and books. Nonetheless, his goal was to create a building that suggested "a smooth cup of Viennese coffee in the afternoon."

To provide a soundtrack for his work and to help him capture the right mood for the Newman Center's various learning and performance spaces, Childress asked Docksey to supply a selection of compositions. Docksey agreed, offering everything from Beethoven to John Cage, whose work can conjure the cacophony of the practice room. Childress also attended music classes to witness the interaction between faculty and students. "I think he always saw buildings as living organisms, and that's what I really admired," Docksey recalled. "It wasn't just the building's size, shape, and footprint that mattered, but instead it was what happened on the inside … as if the building was inhaling and exhaling."

Docksey matched Childress' own passion note for note. During construction, Docksey spent most of his waking hours on-site, making sure that the hardwood floors in the practice rooms were positioned just right and ensuring that the soundproofing in the walls would permit no distractions. Docksey also insisted that each of the forty teaching studios had incandescent, or performance, lighting, as well as twelve-foot ceilings conducive to rich volume and vibrating hardwood floors to create the sense of being on stage. As current DU Provost Gregg Kvistad, then dean of the Arts, Humanities, and Social Sciences, recalled, Docksey's attention to detail never wavered. "I think Joe spent probably more time on that building than anyone, apart from the general contractor. He was just intensely concerned that everything went right," he said.

The finished Newman Center is actually five buildings, each with its own foundation and each separated by a two-inch acoustic dead space designed to keep sound from reverberating from one venue to another. One of the building's signature spaces is the five-level Virginia E. Trevorrow Hall, the academic wing of the center. Trevorrow Hall includes four state-of-the-art classrooms; rehearsal spaces for orchestra, opera/chorus, and jazz; a professional digital recording studio; a music lab; a library; and several virtual practice rooms.

The $67 million Newman Center also features the 1,000-seat June Swaner Gates Concert Hall, designed for opera and large ensembles. The 240-seat Frederic C. Hamilton Family Recital Hall includes a 2,500-pipe Schuke Orgelbau Berlin organ. To optimize and control the quality of sound in both halls, Childress and Docksey solicited the expertise of Kirkegaard Associates, world-class acousticians with offices in Chicago and Boulder.

A third venue, the 350-seat Elizabeth Eriksen Byron Theater, offers flexible space for dramatic productions and an innovative teaching resource for faculty in the theater program, long accustomed to the inflexible stage in Margery Reed Hall. Modeled after the Cottesloe Theatre at London's famed Royal National Theatre in England, the Byron has forty-two stage configurations, created by Davy Davis, chair of the university's theater department. In its first five years in the Byron Theater, Davis noted, the theater program staged seventeen productions using thirteen of the configurations. Unlike the stage in Margery Reed Hall, which took weeks to reconfigure and construct for any given play, the Byron's stage can be transformed in as little as four hours. According to Davis, the modular seating allows for a wide variety of set designs, as well as directing and acting alternatives. "The Byron has allowed us to do shows in ways we could never have imagined prior to the theater being constructed," Davis said.

Before shows and during intermissions, audiences at the three theaters come together in the Joy Burns Plaza, located just inside the building's main entrance off Iliff Avenue. With its terrazzo floor and soaring ceiling, the Joy Burns Plaza also serves as a commons area for music students.

Inside and outside the building, a number of features were added to communicate the building's purpose and to make visitors smile. On the west side of the top floor, a thirteen-foot rose window glows with light late into the night. The building's north side is graced by two twenty-four-foot bas relief carvings representing jazz and classical music. At the west-side entrance, a handful of larger-than-life limestone street performers suggest the commedia dell'arte. A large sundial on the building's south side tells the time of day, though it does not adjust for daylight savings time.

Surveying the Lamont School of Music's home, Docksey counts it a resounding success. "I want new students to our program to be able to hear their footsteps echo when they enter and be in awe and think, 'I can't believe I just made it into this music school,'" he said. "The building definitely creates that sense of wonder."

AN EXTERIOR BAS RELIEF SCULPTURE
TELLS PASSERSBY THEY ARE OUTSIDE A
MUSIC SCHOOL. JOE DOCKSEY, DIRECTOR
OF THE LAMONT SCHOOL OF MUSIC,
TOOK A PASSIONATE INTEREST IN THE
DESIGN OF THE REHEARSAL SPACES,
ONE OF WHICH IS PICTURED AT LEFT.
DOCKSEY INSISTED ON HIGH CEILINGS
AND HARDWOOD FLOORS: "THERE IS
A VIBRATING ASPECT TO HARDWOOD
FLOORS THAT YOU DON'T GET WITH
TILE. IT'S THAT FEELING THAT YOU'RE
ALWAYS ON STAGE." BECAUSE MUSICIANS
ADAPT THEIR PERFORMANCE TO THE
SPACE AND STAGE THEY OCCUPY, IT'S
ALL TOO EASY TO BUILD REHEARSAL
SPACES THAT ENCOURAGE BAD HABITS.

THE NEWMAN CENTER'S ROSE WINDOW
SIGNIFIES THE FLOWERS OFFERED TO
PERFORMERS AT THE END OF A SHOW.
IT WAS DRAWN BY RODGERS AND
CAREFULLY EXECUTED BY ONE OF
CHILDRESS' FAVORITE STONEMASONS.

THE NEWMAN CENTER WAS DESIGNED
TO OFFER THE COMMUNITY FACILITIES
NOT AVAILABLE ELSEWHERE IN DENVER.
ITS STATE-OF-THE-ART RECITAL HALLS
AND THEATERS ALSO PROVIDE DU
STUDENTS THE OPPORTUNITY TO
MASTER THEIR ART FORM.

DANIEL L.
RITCHIE

In any history of the University of Denver, the Daniel L. Ritchie years merit a volume of their own, with whole chapters devoted to his vision, his philosophy, his largesse, and his initiatives. In any narrative of the sixteenth chancellor's eventful life, DU figures just as prominently, testing his resourcefulness, demanding his best efforts, and staking its claim on his affections.

Between 1989 and 2005, Ritchie steered the university through numerous challenges, most notably a $500 million building campaign. Throughout the design and construction processes, he insisted on buildings that would honor the landscape and reflect the culture of a pioneering West. According to university architect Mark Rodgers, Ritchie also wanted buildings that would convey the DU narrative. "I see in these buildings Dan's storytelling influence," he said.

Those who have known him for years say Ritchie's essential traits and preoccupations have been a constant over the decades. "I first met Dan Ritchie about 1960 or 1961," longtime DU trustee Joy Burns told the *University of Denver Magazine* in 2005. "He was, obviously, quite a young man at that time. He was president and CEO of Columbia Savings & Loan, and even back then he had a vision of how things ought to be done. He was that eager, hard-driving, hard-working young man who wanted to give back to the community."

More than that, he was also confident about his priorities and secure in his values. "I don't think that I have ever known a man who is more at peace with who he is," Burns said. That's not to say that he ever lingers in rest mode, she added. "He never stops trying to make things better, and I don't think he ever will."

The son of a North Carolina farm implement dealer, Ritchie earned a bachelor's degree and an MBA from Harvard. After leaving Harvard, he briefly served in the Army and then as a securities analyst in New York. He came to Colorado to run Columbia Savings & Loan in the 1960s.

His next stop was Hollywood, where he served as executive vice president of MCA and worked with the entertainment community's biggest stars. But Hollywood's culture — which he described as "grubby" — left him queasy, and in 1970, he walked away from the glamour and power to test his entrepreneurial skills in the organic food business. That was followed by a thirteen-year stint at Westinghouse Broadcasting, eight years of which he served as CEO.

Ritchie retired at age 55 to his Kremmling spread, the Grand River Ranch, where he planned to spend years, if not the rest of his life, raising cattle and enjoying his patch of

big sky. He was doing just that when, in 1989, he was lured back to Denver to take on problem-plagued DU, whose board of trustees he had joined in 1983. At the time he was asked to become chancellor, Ritchie recalled, "we were borrowing money to make payroll.

"Everywhere you looked, there were problems," Ritchie added. "Clearly, nothing had been done in many years, as there was a significant amount of deferred maintenance. We all knew what we wanted to see, but we didn't know whether we could do it or not."

In 1994, unable to see how momentum could be sustained without a sizable cash infusion, Ritchie gave the university a large portion of his ranch, the sale of which netted DU $15 million. Not long thereafter, he presented the university with the rest of the spread, for a total gift of $50 million.

"Part of the reason was that we needed to do things," he explained. "But part of the reason was to demonstrate to myself that I was not hooked on physical things."

While the physical transformation of the campus counts among Ritchie's most notable achievements, he is especially proud of the institution's community focus, its innovative programs, and its culture of collaboration. Under his leadership, DU channeled its energies to being "a great private university dedicated to the public good." It introduced a number of civic engagement initiatives that put the university's human resources to work in the community. The university also launched many cutting-edge academic programs, including the Marsico Initiative, designed to enhance academic intensity in the arts and sciences, and Cherrington Global Scholars, a one-of-a-kind study abroad program that aims to ensure that DU graduates are prepared for the challenges of global citizenship. At Ritchie's urging, the university also modified its admission process for undergraduate students, introducing the Ammi Hyde Interview, a semi-structured meeting in which members of the university community learn about a prospective student's commitment to academics, community, and inclusiveness.

"The satisfaction I have comes from knowing that the quality we're doing in the buildings is just the visible piece of what we've done," he said. "The other things we've done … have all been enormous undertakings. And they could only have happened because we all put our shoulders to the wheel and did them."

"Build thee more stately mansions, O my soul,

As the swift seasons roll! Leave thy low-vaulted past!

Let each new temple, nobler than the last,

Shut thee from heaven with a dome more vast,

Till thou at length art free,

Leaving thine outgrown shell by life's unresting seas!"

The Chambered Nautilus

BY OLIVER WENDELL HOLMES

CHAMBERS CENTER

**Merle Catherine Chambers Center
for the Advancement of Women**

ARCHITECT OF RECORD
Bennett Wagner & Grody Architects

CONTRACTOR
Kiewit Construction

BUDGET
$8.9 million

SQUARE FOOTAGE
32,000

A BUILDING THAT FOSTERS SYNERGY AND GROWTH

At the Merle Catherine Chambers Center for the Advancement of Women, located on the northwest side of campus, women from throughout Colorado come together to study, grow, and exchange ideas. Home to the University of Denver Women's College, the Chambers Center also provides space for a host of community organizations focused on women's issues, including the Women's Foundation of Colorado and Higher Education Resource Services, a group dedicated to helping women advance in higher education.

The two driving forces behind the development of the 32,000-square-foot Chambers Center, which opened in 2004, were philanthropist Merle Catherine Chambers and Michele "Mike" Bloom, dean of the Women's College from 1997 to 2006. A passionate advocate for women's education, Chambers provided the lead donation to make this valuable resource available to Colorado women. For Bloom, the center represented the fulfillment of a long-cherished dream to offer Women's College students an environment especially designed to inspire achievement and cater to their learning styles.

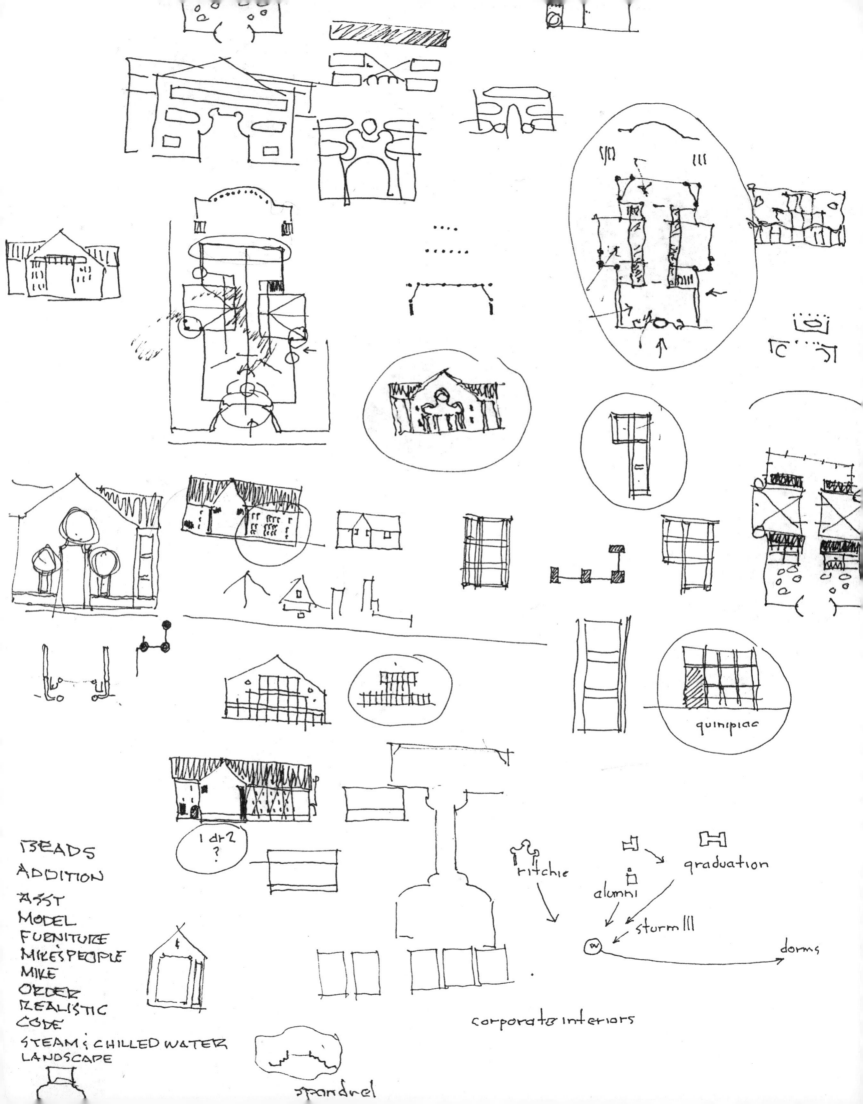

BEADS
ADDITION
ASST
MODEL
FURNITURE
MIKES PEOPLE
MIKE
ORDER
REALISTIC
CODE
STEAM & CHILLED WATER
LANDSCAPE

1 dr 2
?

quinipiac

ritchie

alumni

graduation

storm lll

dorms

corporate interiors

spandrel

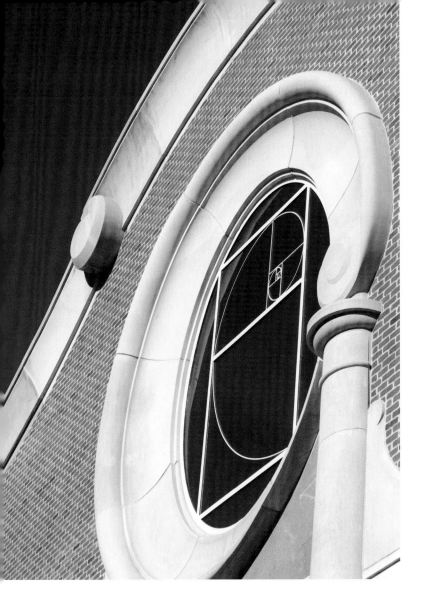

The center became a construction priority with the sale of the Park Hill campus, home to the Women's College for many years. When Bloom began working with architect Jane Loefgren, a protégé of Childress', she envisioned a building designed by women, funded by women, and built by women—all for the benefit of women, thus embodying the Women's College's mission: Women helping women. Bloom's goal was simple: create a comfortable, relaxed, open, and beautiful atmosphere that encourages women to gather and connect on a personal, rather than formal, level.

Arriving at a design that expressed those goals proved, at first, elusive. Heeding Bloom's call to create something "dynamic, organic, natural, and flowing," Loefgren crafted a design featuring oval shapes above the entranceway and columns. The concept was appealing, but not quite right. "Finally," Bloom recalled, "one afternoon while we were in my office collaborating, I picked up a ceramic dish on my desk that I had bought at the Chelsea Crafts Fair in England. Beside it was a glass paperweight with embedded spiral forms suggesting a nautilus shell. Probably not so coincidentally, I had used the nautilus shell as a way of talking about growth and risk to students in regard to their educational journey."

That got Loefgren thinking—about form, beauty, equality, and perfection. In time, she hit upon the idea of employing the nautilus shape and the patterns of the Golden Mean to shape the spaces of the large front window over the building's entranceway. "Mike thought the idea was great—the nautilus form and how going from chamber to chamber really aligned with the mission of the Women's College and the community organizations who shared space in the building. It just seemed to be a natural fit," Loefgren said.

Such a natural fit, in fact, that nautilus imagery appears throughout the building. It shows up not only in the building's front window but also in furniture commissioned for the common room and in copper plates outside offices.

THE CHAMBERS CENTER'S SIGNATURE IS A CHAMBERED NAUTILUS, REPRESENTING THE GROWTH EXPERIENCES OF A LIFETIME. THE NAUTILUS DESIGN SHOWS UP IN THE BUILDING'S LARGE FRONT WINDOW AND ON COPPER PLATES OUTSIDE OFFICES AND CLASSROOMS. THE BUILDING IS RICH IN ARTISTIC TOUCHES, INCLUDING STONE COLUMNS THAT SUGGEST THE FEMALE FORM. ON PAGE 105, THE GARDEN ROOM OPENS TO A COURTYARD FILLED WITH PLANTS AND ART.

One of Loefgren's next challenges was to make the new building blend into the surrounding neighborhood, characterized by one- and two-story bungalows and cottages. "We wanted to create a residential feel … a transition from the neighborhood to the campus to soften it a little bit," Loefgren explained.

Because it incorporates DU's signature materials — red brick, limestone, and copper — the building is immediately identifiable as a university structure. But Loefgren and landscape designer Charles Rapp took steps to make it seem residential as well. On its west elevation, which faces the neighborhood, the building is set back several feet from the street, allowing for landscaping that humanizes its scale. To complement the surrounding homes, Bloom insisted upon plants found in Colorado gardens — shrub roses, tall grasses, and vegetation native to the state.

Childress, who acted as a consultant on the Chambers Center project, pushed Loefgren to play with the building's mood and texture, suggesting that she look to the Church of San Spirito in Florence, Italy, for inspiration. Loefgren drew upon Brunelleschi's celebrated church in placing the Chambers Center's large front window and in incorporating elegant, feminine curves and columns into the exterior. Childress' small pencil sketches of San Spirito helped Loefgren create a simple, open, and accessible design, from the light-infused front foyer on the building's south side, with its fireplace and reception lounge, to the multipurpose garden room on the north side.

With San Spirito still in mind, Loefgren stacked the classrooms on the first and second floor in a cruciform shape. She included operable windows on the building's east and west sides to offer cross breezes for ventilation. Loefgren also made extensive use of glass in the interests of transparency, of creating an open environment in which people can connect easily.

Outside and inside, the building boasts numerous details that make it distinctive. On the north side of the center, stylized columns call to mind the shape of a woman. One of the building's stonemasons suggested that the columns incorporate etched female faces that gaze upon the garden's back wall, which showcases a limestone bas relief sculpture by Kathi Caricof and Madeline Weiner. On the western side of the building, a stained-glass window by artist Sharon Anhorn brings soft light into one of the classrooms. Indoors, an inviting staircase spirals from the first floor to the third, a fitting metaphor for the winding journey of a college education.

IN ADDITION TO HOUSING THE WOMEN'S COLLEGE, THE CHAMBERS CENTER IS HOME TO A NUMBER OF GROUPS DEDICATED TO WOMEN'S EDUCATION AND WELFARE. THEY COME TOGETHER IN LOBBY AND SITTING AREAS, WHERE THEY CAN CAPITALIZE ON BRIGHT LIGHT AND CHEERY DÉCOR. WHEN DESIGNING CLASSROOMS, ARCHITECT JANE LOEFGREN EMPHASIZED FLEXIBILITY AND COMFORT, PARTICULARLY SINCE WOMEN'S COLLEGE CLASSES TYPICALLY LAST FOR FOUR HOURS.

THE DESIGN FOR THE CHAMBERS
CENTER EMPHASIZES TRANSPARENCY
BY DRAWING LIGHT INTO THE BUILDING
THROUGH LARGE WINDOWS. THE
FACILITY ALSO PAYS TRIBUTE TO THE
CREATIVE ACCOMPLISHMENTS OF
WOMEN BY PROVIDING GALLERY
SPACES IN HALLWAYS AND BY
INCORPORATING SCULPTURE INTO THE
GARDEN. THE DOORWAY TO THE
GARDEN ROOM IS FLANKED BY DISPLAY
CASES, ANOTHER OPPORTUNITY TO
SHOWCASE ART.

A SPIRAL STAIRCASE CALLS TO MIND THE
CHAMBERED NAUTILUS. AT BETWEEN-FLOORS
LANDINGS, STUDENTS CAN LINGER AT A
WINDOW SEAT TO CHAT WITH A CLASSMATE
OR PONDER THE VIEW TO THE EAST.

Whenever possible, the University of Denver has restored its historic structures and adapted its existing stock to modern uses. The first building constructed on campus, University Hall, serves as beacon for campus visitors. Across campus at refurbished Sturm Hall, DU students come together in a bright, modern setting for classes in the humanities and social sciences. In Craig Hall, a once dim and sterile residence building takes on new life as a center for innovative social work.

ADAPTING OLD BUILDINGS FOR NEW PURPOSES

5

STURM HALL

"Our job is to bring light into dim places. It's not a matter of tearing things down."

— G. CABELL CHILDRESS

TO BRING HISTORIC GEMS AND HARD-WORKING TWENTIETH-CENTURY BUILDINGS UP-TO-DATE, THE UNIVERSITY'S DESIGN TEAM EMBARKED ON A SERIES OF RENOVATIONS THAT SOUGHT TO HONOR THE PAST WHILE ANTICIPATING THE FUTURE. THE TEAM BEGAN WITH UNIVERSITY HALL, PICTURED ON PAGE 110, AND CONTINUED WITH CRAIG HALL, SHOWN AT THE TOP OF THIS PAGE, AND STURM HALL, AT LEFT.

A HISTORIC STRUCTURE GETS A MODERN MAKEOVER

On university campuses across the United States, old buildings lend character to their settings. They speak to enduring values and traditions.

At the University of Denver, the nineteenth century is represented by University Hall, once known as Old Main. With its solidity and solemnity, it symbolizes the institution's resilience through decades of triumphs and tribulations.

UNIVERSITY HALL

University Hall

ARCHITECT OF RECORD
Davis Partnership

CONTRACTOR
Shaw Construction

BUDGET
$3.5 million

SQUARE FOOTAGE
42,000

By the 1990s, the building was sorely in need of an update. That update was especially critical because the building has traditionally been the first structure that visitors to campus encounter. Housing the Office of Admission, the Office of the Registrar, and University College, it assumes a high-profile role in student recruitment and student services. Consequently, the building needs to make a good impression. The challenge was to restore its former glory while incorporating a twenty-first century aesthetic and to update it without imposing new sensibilities.

Before its overhaul, University Hall looked every bit of its 104 years, both inside and out. Thanks to a lack of routine maintenance, the building was crumbling. Cracked walls, a leaky roof, peeling paint, a dirt-floor basement, and a surrounding landscape choked with weeds — all combined to make the building a candidate for the wrecking ball. "Clearly, people did not respect it," Dan Ritchie remembered. Consequently, the building's makeover was at the top of his to-do list after he became chancellor.

WHEN IT WAS FIRST CONSTRUCTED, UNIVERSITY HALL SERVED AS THE INSTITUTION'S ADMINISTRATIVE AND ACADEMIC HEADQUARTERS. A HUNDRED YEARS AFTER ITS DEBUT, THE BUILDING WAS IN DIRE NEED OF A MAKEOVER. WITH A $3.5 MILLION BUDGET, THE DESIGN TEAM SOUGHT TO PREPARE THE BUILDING FOR A NEW CENTURY WHILE PRESERVING ITS ARCHITECTURAL CHARACTER.

SPORTING A NEW COPPER ROOF AND UPDATED INFRASTRUCTURE, UNIVERSITY HALL PLAYS A VITAL ROLE IN THE LIFE OF THE CAMPUS. IT HOUSES THE OFFICE OF ADMISSION, MAKING IT AN ESSENTIAL STOP FOR PROSPECTIVE STUDENTS VISITING CAMPUS.

115

Renovating and adapting any historic building requires not only architectural savvy, but also extreme patience and a belief that the past deserves respect. On that note, Cab Childress was fond of quoting one of his early mentors: "Learn architecture, not style, in order to do the right thing in the right place while respecting what has been done in the past."

For Childress, University Hall represented more than just stone walls and a roof. It was an example of architectural ingenuity by Robert Roeschlaub, its original designer. Childress was especially appreciative of University Hall's rhyolite and sandstone exterior. The rustic materials had, for the most part, aged gracefully, withstanding a century of punishing Colorado weather.

Working with a slender budget of $3.5 million, Childress assembled the team that would ready this building for the twenty-first century: Mark Rodgers, longtime associate Keith Connor, and Brian Erickson of Davis Partnership, the architect of record. Among other improvements, the team set contractors to work repairing broken stone, patching the cracks in the mortar, reconstructing any load-bearing walls that were deemed unsafe, and installing a massive HVAC unit. They also had all the windows replaced and the building's cupola refurbished to its former luster. To protect the building from the elements, they topped it with a copper roof, which blended with the rhyolite and sandstone, as well as with the campus' new construction. Finally, the team added a new north entrance with a stone façade to make University Hall wheelchair accessible. In doing so, they adhered as much as possible to the flavor and feel of the rest of the building. "Cab did not want to pretend that Roeschlaub had designed this addition, but instead, he wanted to create a piece that showed care and appreciation about how Roeschlaub put the original building together," Rodgers said.

Whenever possible, Childress incorporated the materials that Roeschlaub used, including rhyolite quarried from the same pit that produced the original rock. Childress purposely left the new stonework at the north entry clean, largely to acknowledge where Roeschlaub's work ended and the new work began. However, during construction some of the original stone was damaged, so Childress had the new rhyolite patch treated with a combination of oil, cigarette ashes, and Colorado dirt, ensuring that it matched, as closely as possible, the century-old existing rock. Today, many discerning eyes cannot spot where old stone ends and the new stone patch begins.

ON PAGE 116, A COPPER RELIEF
BY ARTIST SHARON ANHORN
INCORPORATES THE UNIVERSITY'S
SEAL AND TOPS THE NORTH
ENTRANCE TO THE BUILDING. THE
ENTRANCE WAS ADDED DURING
RENOVATIONS TO ADDRESS
ACCESSIBILITY ISSUES FOR THE
DISABLED. THE BUILDING'S STONE
CONSTRUCTION AND ARTISTIC
DETAILS MAKE IT A FAVORITE AMONG
STUDENTS. INSIDE, WINDING
STAIRCASES ANCHOR THE EAST AND
WEST ENDS OF THE BUILDING. THE
HANDCRAFTED WOODEN BANISTERS
CONTRIBUTE TO THE INTERIOR'S
PERIOD FEEL.

The building's interior required just as much work as its exterior. Even though it had received some updates in 1979, the structure was in dire need of attention. The floorboards on the two grand staircases creaked with each footstep, valuable open space had been filled with offices, and the paint was peeling off the walls. In addition, without an infrastructure overhaul to support new technology, the offices were unsuited to modern applications.

New carpeting and a fresh coat of paint did much to freshen the interior, and the new windows allowed bright sunshine to flow into the corridors and offices. Perhaps the biggest difference was created by the addition of handcrafted wooden banisters and chair rails, carefully detailed by Brian Erickson. The banisters punctuate the building's pleasing curves, making a climb up the stairs seem an enticing alternative to the elevator. The chair rails, meanwhile, call to mind the building's origins in a long-gone time.

Childress' revisions and renovations to University Hall gave the venerable old building a well-deserved second chance at relevance. Today, it is one of the most important structures on campus, housing offices whose day-to-day work touches every student and faculty member.

The building's workhorse status delights Rodgers. On another campus, a building like University Hall might have been relegated to relic status. "We're not in the business of running a museum," Rodgers said. "University Hall is what a university is all about. It cherishes its past while trying to find ways to serve its future."

DURING ITS FIRST CENTURY OF USE, UNIVERSITY HALL ENDURED PERIODIC UPDATES THAT CHOPPED UP THE OPEN SPACES AND FILLED THEM WITH OFFICES. ONE OF THE DESIGN TEAM'S FIRST TASKS WAS TO RESTORE A COMFORTABLE FLOW TO THE INTERIOR SPACES AND PROVIDE ROOMS FOR MULTIPLE PURPOSES. FOR EXAMPLE, A THIRD-FLOOR CLASSROOM, SUPPORTING AUDIO-VISUAL TECHNOLOGY, CAN DOUBLE AS A MEETING ROOM.

BUCHTEL
BUNGALOW

Between 1906 and his death in 1924, Henry Augustus Buchtel, who served as university chancellor from 1899 to 1920, made his home in a comfortable bungalow at 2100 South Columbine Street, just blocks from the campus he loved. In the early years of the century, the pasture across the street supported the Buchtel family's Jersey cow, though that bucolic space soon made way for elegant homes.

Designed by architect Harlan Thomas, the two-story craftsman-style bungalow has played a celebrated role in university and Colorado history. During Buchtel's tenure as chancellor, the bungalow was opened to faculty and students for periodic Thursday afternoon teas. The bungalow doubled as the governor's mansion from 1907 through 1909, when Buchtel served as Colorado's highest elected official.

In 1927, the university purchased the home from Buchtel's daughter for $10 and the balance of a $6,000 loan. During World War II, the bungalow was used as a dining facility for female students living with nearby families. In the sixty years since then, it has served as a faculty men's club, a faculty rental property, a female graduate student residence, and as a home for the Women's Library Association.

At one point, the university proposed turning the 2,792-square-foot dwelling into a bed and breakfast, but that idea was quashed by the University Park Neighborhood Association. In 2004, the university put the home up for sale, but offers on the property were disappointing.

Finally, in 2005, Chancellor Robert Coombe suggested that the Buchtel Bungalow be remodeled to provide a home for the university's chief officer. "When I became chancellor, it was on the market and almost surely would have been demolished by a buyer or developer. Our motivation was to save it," Coombe said.

Campus architect Jane Loefgren took on the daunting task, providing designs to shore up the building's foundation while converting it from an architectural artifact to a modern residence. When the Buchtel Bungalow was built, it had a coal furnace, enclosed "tuberculosis" porch, wood-fired kitchen stove, a hutch for chickens, and a shed for cows. The interior had a coffered ceiling with fir beams and a brick tile fireplace flanked by built-in bookshelves. Extra bookshelves lined the room's perimeter along with a plate rail on which Buchtel displayed his lavish cup and saucer collection.

Today, the bungalow has a new granite kitchen, updated bathrooms, restored fir floors, a new cedar-shingle roof, and modern electrical, plumbing, and heating systems. It also has a new two-car garage and insulated double-pane windows that match the originals.

Coombe and his wife, Julanna Gilbert, moved into the historic home in August 2007. It was originally listed on the National Register of Historic Places in 1989.

UPDATING THE MODERN

When it opened on the north side of campus in the 1960s, Sturm Hall, then known as the General Classroom Building, was regarded as a modern edifice that would keep pace with rapidly changing times. It wasn't long before the building's learning spaces became outdated — aesthetically and technologically. Just three decades after it opened, the building demanded a major renovation.

S T U R M   H A L L

Sturm Hall

ARCHITECT OF RECORD
Root Rosenman Architects LLP

CONTRACTOR
Gerald H. Phipps Inc.

BUDGET
$5 million

SQUARE FOOTAGE
177,000

With its many classrooms of varied sizes, Sturm Hall has long been one of DU's most used buildings. A contemporary of Cherrington Hall and the Boettcher Center, both located on the south side of campus, it was constructed in expedient fashion to handle a burgeoning student population. What it lacked in charm and intimacy, it made up for in its ability to handle large numbers of students. In the late 1980s and until construction was completed on the Daniels College of Business, it served as a hub for business students.

In 1997, two years before the business school moved out of the building, alumnus Donald Sturm and his wife, Susan, gave the university a sizable gift to remodel the structure as a home for the humanities and social sciences programs. At the time, the programs were scattered in assorted buildings across campus. Thanks to this incoherent arrangement, faculty and students had too few opportunities to interact and engage in cross-disciplinary work.

IN THE 1960s, THE NEWLY CONSTRUCTED
GENERAL CLASSROOM BUILDING INTRODUCED
MODERN ARCHITECTURE TO THE NORTH SIDE
OF CAMPUS. THE BUILDING OFFERED MANY
CLASSROOMS OF VARYING SIZES, MAKING IT
A BUSY CROSSROADS FOR STUDENTS.

THE MULTIMILLION-DOLLAR RENOVATION OF THE
GENERAL CLASSROOM BUILDING TRANSFORMED
IT INTO STURM HALL, A HUB FOR STUDENTS
MAJORING IN THE HUMANITIES AND SOCIAL
SCIENCES. CHANGES TO THE BUILDING BROUGHT
IT INTO THE TWENTY-FIRST CENTURY, WITH
SMART-TO-THE-SEAT CLASSROOMS, ENHANCED
TECHNOLOGY, AND PLENTY OF SPACES DESIGNED
TO FOSTER INTERACTION AMONG STUDENTS
AND PROFESSORS.

News of the Sturm donation delighted Roscoe Hill, then dean of the Divisions of Arts, Humanities, and Social Sciences. Finally, his students would have a central home, a place where they could meet and greet their peers from other programs in the hallways. This simple interaction would enhance the student experience considerably. But pleased as he was, Hill had reservations. Could the $5 million remodeling budget even make a dent in the long and ever-growing list of necessary repairs and renovations?

Any concerns were immediately quelled after his first meeting with the design team: Childress, associate Jane Loefgren, and representatives from the architect of record, Root Rosenman Architects LLP.

Hill's introduction to Childress' often-eccentric approach stands out in his memory. "I told Cab during our first-ever meeting that Sturm Hall was a big building, and we had *only* $5 million to work with," Hill recalled. "He then told me to spin around 360 degrees in the swivel chair I was sitting in and face him again, which I did. He then said, 'OK, now you're in a new world.'"

Not surprisingly, that new world had its own limitations —largely the result of the way the building was originally designed and constructed. An assessment of the building revealed that the floor of one classroom was the ceiling of its counterpart a floor below. That fact, along with several other curiosities, made structural changes difficult.

According to current DU Provost Gregg Kvistad, who succeeded Hill as dean of the Arts, Humanities, and Social Sciences, Sturm Hall's redesign was intended to "provide a home for as many departments as possible and create a physical community for the arts, humanities, and social sciences." Aesthetically pleasing wall paneling and warm paint colors were introduced to counter the sterility of tiered lecture-style classrooms. In addition, Childress added breakout rooms, so student teams could collaborate on special projects. Finally, the office areas for professors were enlarged, providing inviting space for outside-the-classroom interaction with students.

To prepare the building for the reality of twenty-first century education, the infrastructure needed a massive update. Plans called for nine smart-to-the-seat classrooms, where students and professors could plug in their laptops and explore the cyber world. In addition, almost all of the classrooms required DVD, VCR, and PowerPoint technology. A host of laboratories also needed flexible furnishings and access to advanced technology.

By the time this work was done, the budget was nearly exhausted. Unfortunately, not every item on Hill's wish list was delivered. He laments, most of all, that limited funds prevented inclusion of an on-site coffee shop conducive to after-class conversations. Still, Hill noted, the building has enhanced teaching capabilities, allowing professors to modernize, even revolutionize, the way they share ideas and promote discourse. What's more, the new Sturm Hall stands as a high-profile home for programs once relegated to the hinterlands.

STURM HALL'S DAVIS AUDITORIUM, SHOWN AT THE TOP OF PAGE 125, WELCOMES GUEST LECTURERS THROUGHOUT THE ACADEMIC YEAR. THE SPACE OUTSIDE THE AUDITORIUM ALLOWS FOR MINGLING AND SMOOTH TRAFFIC FLOW.

THE RENOVATION OF STURM HALL
AIMED TO GIVE STUDENTS A BRIGHT,
CHEERFUL, AND TECHNOLOGICALLY
UP-TO-DATE SPACE FOR LEARNING.
THE DESIGN TEAM ALSO WORKED TO
CREATE OFFICE SPACE THAT PROFESSORS
COULD MAKE THEIR OWN AND COULD
USE FOR CREATIVE AND SCHOLARLY
WORK. FOR EXAMPLE, IN POET BIN
RAMKE'S OFFICE, SHOWN AT RIGHT,
BOOKS AND PLANTS COMBINE TO
PROVIDE THE INSPIRATION NECESSARY
FOR COMPOSITION.

TO THE WEST OF STURM HALL, AN
OUTDOOR CLASSROOM GETS PLENTY
OF USE WHEN WEATHER PERMITS.
SITUATED OFF THE BEATEN PATH, THE
SPACE OFFERS PRIVACY AND QUIET.

THE UGLY DUCKLING BECOMES A SWAN

Childress believed in loving a building — any building — regardless of its age and appearance. But Spruce Hall, the predecessor of today's Rebecca T. and James P. Craig Hall, was hard to love.

"The building was the pits. It was disgraceful … horrible," said Catherine Alter, who served as dean of the Graduate School of Social Work (GSSW) from 1996 to 2006. GSSW had long occupied the building, constructed to house the influx of

CRAIG HALL

Rebecca T. and James P. Craig Hall

ARCHITECT OF RECORD
Andrews & Anderson Architects

CONTRACTOR
Mortenson

BUDGET
$11 million

SQUARE FOOTAGE
54,000

students enrolling after World War II. The social work community made the most of Spruce Hall's array of cramped bedrooms, bathrooms, and closets, adapting the improbable space for classrooms and offices. One large and two small classrooms were in the basement, the only open space available, but these had minimal ventilation and reverberated with the sounds of toilets flushing from above. Upstairs, faculty and staff offices were wedged between thirty-eight bathrooms on four floors. With exposed water lines running throughout each room and with little natural light, the facilities were cramped and cheerless. In 1996, after touring the building with Alter, Ritchie adopted her conviction that GSSW needed greatly improved facilities.

The question facing Ritchie and Alter was whether to tear down Spruce Hall and start fresh or renovate and improve the 36,000-square-foot building. Ultimately, Rodgers recalled, the decision came down to practical considerations. With an $11 million budget, the university could build a new structure of roughly 35,000 square feet. Or, it could use that same money to rehabilitate the old building and incorporate an 18,000-square-foot addition, giving the social work program 54,000 square feet for its expanding ambitions.

FOR DECADES, THE GRADUATE SCHOOL
OF SOCIAL WORK WAS HOUSED IN
DILAPIDATED SPRUCE HALL, A FORMER
RESIDENCE FACILITY FOR SOLDIERS
RETURNING FROM WORLD WAR II. IN
RE-IMAGINING THE BUILDING, THE
DESIGN TEAM WORKED WITH SEVERAL
DIFFERENT RENDERINGS, EACH
INCORPORATING AN ADDITION THAT
DRAMATICALLY CHANGED THE
BUILDING'S EXTERIOR. THE TEAM
BELIEVED THAT, BY MAKING MAXIMUM
USE OF AVAILABLE RESOURCES TO
CREATE BEAUTIFUL AND USEFUL SPACE,
THEY WERE PAYING TRIBUTE TO THE
CHALLENGES FACING SOCIAL WORKERS,
WHO TYPICALLY MUST ACCOMPLISH A
GREAT DEAL WITH VERY LITTLE.

CATHERINE ALTER, FORMER DEAN OF THE GRADUATE SCHOOL OF SOCIAL WORK, CREDITS THE RENOVATION AND ADDITION WITH GIVING SOCIAL WORK STUDENTS A WORTHY SETTING FOR THEIR SCHOLARSHIP AND CLINICAL WORK. TODAY, SOCIAL WORKERS FROM THROUGHOUT THE REGION REGARD THE BUILDING AS A CENTER FOR LEARNING AND PLANNING.

The renovation scheme looked promising on paper, but it wasn't convincing to every DU decision maker. Members of the building and grounds committee questioned the validity of remodeling instead of starting over. "Are you sure you want to do this?" they asked Rodgers prior to giving project approval. "Is it wise to spend this much money remodeling rather than building?"

For Rodgers, answering that question was not easy. "Our mission," he said, "was to maximize value out of the extra square footage and thereby ensure the new structure supported GSSW's program and what it wanted to have." What ultimately saved the building — "the tipping point," as Rodgers called it — was the window count. As a former residence building with plenty of bedrooms, Spruce Hall had the windows to serve a new configuration that included lots of offices.

The decision to remodel was welcome news to Childress. "I look at buildings as people," he told an interviewer in 2006. "The decision of whether or not to demolish a building is a moral question, and I find no pleasure in it."

Childress also believed that any project — whether new construction or a renovation — should focus on the needs and spirits of the structure's occupants. He found a kindred spirit in Alter, who insisted that every aspect of the project benefit students, faculty, staff, and the community.

The job of financing the project was given a boost by prominent GSSW alumna Rebecca Craig and her husband, James. Securing a generous contribution from the Craigs' foundation made a huge difference. After all, GSSW, like most social work programs, could not count on a stable of wealthy alumni to underwrite its campaigns. Although they give generously, social workers seldom earn enough to make sizable contributions.

With fundraising underway, Childress assigned the renovation to Rodgers and his longtime colleague, Bill Campbell. The architect of record was Andrews & Anderson. Working closely with Alter — who, Campbell recalled, "would not give an inch on her building"— the team crafted a design that emphasized flexibility and that included a number of features critical to the program's long-term viability. To remain competitive in national rankings and to attract a new generation of highly qualified students, GSSW needed—and got—five technologically up-to-date classrooms, comfortable offices, a virtual library, five break-out rooms, two student lounges, and two clinical training suites where students can observe clinical interventions. A large commons room was designed to accommodate formal and informal gatherings, while an outdoor terrace with seating was created to promote relaxed interaction. To erase any last trace of Spruce Hall's gloomy appearance, the architects introduced a series of stained-glass art windows by Chicago artist Larry Zgoda. These filter eastern light into the commons room, the meeting rooms, and a student lounge.

Since Craig Hall's opening in 2005, the social work program has risen dramatically in the *U.S. News & World Report* rankings — validating Alter's insistence that all the improvements yield tangible benefits for faculty and staff. "Catherine was a great owner," Rodgers said. "She made sure there were things in that building that I may never have thought of or that Andrews & Anderson may not have remembered. That's part of what made this building fresh and different and what gave it its own uniqueness. ... And regarding our belief in sustainability, what a wonderful thing not to have had to tear down this building and consign it to a landfill. By renovating, restoring, and adding on, we have, hopefully, given this program the use of this building for another hundred years."

Once the building opened, Alter saw an immediate change in the morale of GSSW students and professors. "The students loved coming to class, and the faculty came to work with smiles on their faces," she said. "For the students, it was a message that they were not second-class citizens and were just as important as the law or business school students. Craig Hall also brought the Colorado professional social work community together by providing a remarkable home for learning and planning. I just cannot put into words the amazing change in the culture and attitude of everyone associated with GSSW."

That was largely the result of the collaboration between Alter and the team of architects assigned to the project. Under Alter's guidance, Rodgers and Campbell worked to emphasize community engagement in their design, putting the high-ceilinged community room just inside the front door, where no visitor to the building could miss it. They did so to honor the critical role that social workers play in the community, and they did so despite the structural limitations of the existing building. In fact, it required outside-the-box — "or in this case," Rodgers said, "outside-the-truss" — thinking to incorporate the expansive space into a low-ceilinged building originally designed for the sole purpose of sheltering students.

Just as important, Alter added, the entire team embodied Childress' commitment to serving the building's occupants. "Cab cared about the *people* more than he cared about the building. It was people and their needs and dreams that came first."

STAINED-GLASS WINDOWS, WIDE-OPEN HALLWAYS, SECLUDED STUDY AREAS, AND SPACIOUS GATHERING ROOMS COMBINE TO MAKE CRAIG HALL A WARM AND WELCOMING SETTING FOR CLASSES AND RESEARCH.

FLEXIBLE CLASSROOM SPACE HAS PROVED CONDUCIVE
TO TRADITIONAL LECTURES AND CLASS DISCUSSIONS, AS
WELL AS TO COLLABORATIVE PROJECTS. THE ROOMS
ACCOMMODATE SMALL NUMBERS AND LARGE NUMBERS
GRACEFULLY, MAKING IT EASY FOR PROFESSORS TO
CREATE AN INTIMATE ENVIRONMENT WHERE EVERYONE
IS INVITED TO PARTICIPATE.

STUDENT LOUNGE AREAS, PICTURED ABOVE, PROVIDE A COMFORTABLE RESPITE FROM THE CHALLENGES OF THE CLASSROOM. THE WARM COLORS USED THROUGHOUT THE BUILDING REINFORCE THE PROGRAM'S EMPHASIS ON COLLEGIALITY.

When work began in fall 1999 on the schematics for the Frank H. Ricketson Jr. Law Building, the architects and owners committed to a plan that would make wise use of natural resources for the benefit of the university's human resources. The result is a building that embodies the Sturm College of Law's environmental ethos while providing healthy and pleasant spaces for learning.

BUILDING GREEN

6

"I just like materials. I like real materials. What should a university be if not real and honest?"

— G. CABELL CHILDRESS

NATURAL LIGHT FILLS THE MAIN COMMON AREA INSIDE THE RICKETSON LAW BUILDING, REDUCING THE BUILDING'S RELIANCE ON ELECTRIC LIGHTING. THE DESIGN TEAM WORKED WITH THE STURM COLLEGE OF LAW'S BUILDING COMMITTEE TO CREATE A "TOWN SQUARE" ENVIRONMENT THAT WOULD REMIND STUDENTS ABOUT THE ROLE LAW PLAYS IN CIVIC SOCIETY.

DEPARTING FROM THE TRADITIONAL BLUEPRINTS

In the past decade, a number of law schools have moved into new buildings. But only one law school — the University of Denver Sturm College of Law — has moved into a structure quite like the Frank H. Ricketson Jr. Law Building.

RICKETSON LAW BUILDING

Frank H. Ricketson Jr. Law Building

ARCHITECTS OF RECORD
H+L Architecture
Shepley Bulfinch Richardson & Abbott

CONTRACTOR
Saunders Construction

BUDGET
$63.5 million

SQUARE FOOTAGE
242,000

According to Arthur Best, a DU law professor who served as chairman of the building committee during the Ricketson Law Building's gestation, most law schools build structures designed in conjunction with a tried-and-true model: big classrooms to accommodate a hefty enrollment, isolated faculty offices, and a large library where students study in silence and there is little opportunity for collaborative learning.

Named after a prominent alumnus who earned his law degree in 1918, the Ricketson Law Building, which opened in 2003, bucked that trend in numerous ways. It aimed to create a welcoming environment that reflected new ideas about teaching and learning. In addition, it was designed to communicate the law school's values and strengths, particularly its commitment to environmental law programs. It is the first law school in the United States and the first building in Colorado to earn gold certification from the U.S. Green Building Council.

Best and other members of the law school faculty particularly wanted the new facility to complement the school's student-focused culture. With this in mind, they wanted to reduce some of the competitive tension generally associated with pursuit of a law degree. To emphasize collaboration and communication, to create a friendly atmosphere in which students could become friends rather than rivals, the interior includes dozens of spaces created for impromptu conversations or group study sessions. The hallways double as meeting spots, with comfortable chairs grouped here and there. "To me, that is the unique feature of this building," Best said.

Established in 1892, the Denver Law School was organized as a department of the University of Denver. It was originally situated in the Jacob Haish Building in downtown Denver at the corner of 14th and Arapahoe streets, the current site of a Denver Performing Arts Complex parking garage. By all accounts, the facility was nothing special, but it served well enough for nineteen years. After that, the school changed location eight times, setting up shop in a downtown high rise and later on the second floor of the Mapelli Brothers' Grocery and Meat Market at 211 15th Street. Eventually, in 1984, the law program settled in for a twenty-year stay at the Park Hill campus.

From the day he assumed DU's chancellorship, Dan Ritchie was determined to anchor the law school on the University Park campus. While the Park Hill facility was adequate, its physical isolation nearly eight miles away meant that it was difficult for law students to take advantage of the University Park campus' amenities and academic resources. The separation also made it challenging for law faculty to interact with their peers from other programs. What's more, maintaining two campuses represented a financial strain.

Ritchie's plans were rushed into realization when Johnson & Wales University, a school offering courses in business, hospitality, culinary arts, and technology, exercised its option to purchase the remaining portion of the Park Hill campus in September 1999. That move advanced the timeline for vacating the law facilities and breaking ground on a new law center. Suddenly, the university had just three and a half years to design, build, and open a new facility, considerably less than the five years generally required for such a massive undertaking.

By September 1999, Cab Childress had already retired as university architect, a post that Mark Rodgers then assumed. Because talk of a new law school had long been part of Ritchie's vision, DU architect Jane Loefgren and

architectural consultant Bill Campbell, as well as former associate Margie Soo Hoo Lee, were deep into discussions and sketches about the proposed new building. Before the sale of the Park Hill campus, they had conducted joint programming exercises, interviewing law faculty and students about the items on their wish lists for interior spaces. When Johnson & Wales exercised its option to buy, this work proved an enormous time saver. "The clock was not ours at that point," Rodgers recalled.

Perhaps the most notable idea to have emerged from the programming exercises came from an interview with George "Rock" Pring, an environmental law professor active in environmental causes. Prodded by one of his students, Pring suggested that the new law school be built according to the exacting standards of the U.S. Green Building Council's Leadership in Energy and Environmental Design (LEED) certification system. "Back in 2000, when I was on the building committee, a student asked me if we were going to build green. And I must admit, to my embarrassment today, my first response was, 'No, I think it's going to be the red brick color that Chancellor Ritchie likes.'"

Once he learned about building green, Pring was a convert, and he advanced the idea that DU could signal its leadership in the areas of environmental and natural resources law and ethics by "practicing what it teaches."

GREENING THE BUILDING AND GOING FOR GOLD

Sustainable design and construction practices, as well as the use of energy-efficient materials, had always been part of Childress' ethic. The university's preferred building materials—copper roofing, sandstone, limestone, and brick—were chosen as much for their durability as for their aesthetics. What's more, Childress' insistence on double-wall brick construction ensured manageable heating and cooling costs—largely because, Rodgers explained, it keeps the buildings from having to adjust to the temperature of the moment. Childress described it more metaphorically. "We wrap the building in a blanket," he said, noting that this protection can extend the life of a building by centuries. That's in part because the double-wall brick construction has, over the centuries, proved resilient through the hundred-plus freeze-thaw cycles that characterize Denver weather.

Even in the earliest days of his career, Childress paid heed to ecological issues. In addition to favoring durable

THE ARCHITECTURAL TEAM HAD JUST OVER THREE YEARS TO DESIGN AND OVERSEE CONSTRUCTION OF THE RICKETSON LAW BUILDING. TYPICALLY, A PROJECT OF THIS SIZE AND SCOPE REQUIRES FIVE OR MORE YEARS TO COMPLETE. THE CHALLENGE WAS MADE EVEN MORE FORMIDABLE BY THE IMPERATIVE TO BUILD GREEN, WHICH REQUIRED THAT DESIGNERS AND CONTRACTORS EMPLOY NEW PRACTICES, MATERIALS, AND SITE-MANAGEMENT TECHNIQUES.

AT 242,000 SQUARE FEET, THE
RICKETSON LAW BUILDING
REPRESENTS ONE OF THE LARGEST
ACADEMIC STRUCTURES ON
CAMPUS. IT INCORPORATES
RECYCLED STRUCTURAL STEEL
AND MANY MATERIALS THAT
WERE SOURCED LOCALLY. ITS
EXTERIOR LIGHTING WAS
ESPECIALLY DESIGNED TO
MINIMIZE LIGHT POLLUTION.

materials, he consistently worked to make maximum use of natural light. He also chose materials that required little maintenance and minimal use of paint, thus reducing fumes and offgassing. His approach to building, Rodgers said, made Childress one of the earliest green designers, though he never operated under that label. As Loefgren said, "It wasn't called 'green' back then, but that was what it was."

Although Childress' heirs were well-schooled in his approach to responsible building, they had never designed an entire building utilizing LEED standards. LEED allocates points for various benchmarks, including sustainable site management, transportation alternatives, water conservation, energy efficiency, environmentally safe materials, recycling, indoor air-quality control, and innovation in design. By attaining a certain number of points, an organization can achieve Silver, Gold, or Platinum status.

From Pring's perspective, the LEED designations encourage and reward a kind of building that makes economic sense. "When you get right down to it, green building is nothing more than designing buildings that are safe for their occupants and safe for the rest of the environment. It's not some kind of a 'Star Wars' building, but instead it's just good meat and potatoes architecture and equipment," he said.

Besides Loefgren and Rodgers, the project design team included Patrick Johnson of Denver's H+L Architecture, who collaborated with the team of Ralph Jackson, Jan Heespelink, and Geoff Freeman of Boston-based Shepley Bulfinch Richardson & Abbott (SBRA). H+L's experience in designing local civic, corporate, health-care, and educational facilities complemented SBRA's nationally recognized expertise in creating law schools. The final piece of the design puzzle was put in place when internationally recognized environmental architect Greg Franta of Boulder was brought on board. Because H+L had never designed a law school, and SBRA had never completed a green project, their collaboration with Franta was all the more critical.

To build according to green practices, DU hired one of Colorado's largest general contractors, Saunders Construction, headed by Dick Saunders, who graduated from DU in 1963 with a degree in real estate and construction.

Given the project's compressed timeline and ambitious LEED goals, collaboration and communication were essential. Taking a page from Childress' notebook, Loefgren and Rodgers emphasized that all members of the team would need to come together to share ideas and information. Childress had often stressed that "the richness of architecture is the collaboration," and that by respecting the expertise and talents of contractors and craftspeople, the buildings would benefit. He believed strongly in listening to everybody's ideas, and he measured design success by the architect's ability to integrate varying concepts into the mix.

Thanks to this insistence on respect and collaborative work, the expedited timeline was made feasible. "It forced intensity of focus from the faculty, administration, fundraisers, architects, engineers, and contractors," Rodgers said. "Everyone performed their roles with the symphony, and we got the right team."

As the collaborative process advanced, it became apparent that not every member of the College of Law community endorsed the idea of building green. Skeptics feared that the effort would cost too much, take too long, and yield too few tangible results. "Some of them thought I was crazy," Pring recalled.

Undeterred, Pring and Franta took to the front lines to sell the idea. One of their most convincing arguments involved an analysis of long-term savings. The up-front costs associated with building green amounted to about one percent of the total $63.5 million budget. But that was minuscule, Pring explained, when compared to the energy savings that could be realized over the lifetime of the building.

Franta, who helped draft the U.S. Green Building Council's building doctrine, made his arguments on the economic, environmental, and health advantages of green design and construction to a group that included Ritchie, donors Donald and Susan Sturm, the building committee, deans, and faculty members. "When it was all over," Pring recalled, "Dan Ritchie stood up, pointed in Greg's direction and said, 'Hire him and go for gold.'"

FROM SATELLITE TO CENTER STAGE

Although Ritchie was determined that the law school would relocate to the University Park campus, the question of where to site the required new building proved problematic. Ritchie asked Rodgers to identify a handful of sites that could accommodate a large building and then tour the locations with the law school's building committee. The resulting survey of four sites, including one on the far northeast corner of campus, resulted in a judicious weighing of pros and cons. Eventually, the building committee proposed the most central of the locations. That decision, Rodgers explained, proved both beneficial and problematic. On the one hand,

THE KEYSTONES ON THE RICKETSON LAW BUILDING SIGNAL ITS PURPOSE AND ITS LOCATION: "LEX," FOR EXAMPLE, IS THE LATIN DESIGNATION FOR LAW, WHILE A REPRESENTATION OF THE DU LOGO ORIENTS VISITORS TO PLACE.

a central location would reiterate the law school's ties to the University of Denver while testifying to the university's importance to the law school. At the same time, the central location was the smallest of the proposed sites and the most challenging for construction crews.

The building's prominent location, across from the newly remodeled Sturm Hall and adjacent to the Ricks Center for Gifted Children, makes it easily visible from much of campus. Its west-facing windows offer commanding views of the Rocky Mountains, while the building's grand entryway opens onto Campus Green. The fourth-floor corridor runs north-south and aligns with the Buchtel Memorial Chapel on the building's south side. From that floor, an inviting window frames a view of faraway Pikes Peak.

Throughout the building, natural light pours in from windows and a "lightrium" constructed on the roof. This skylight fills the center of the building with the sun's rays, proving the perfect solution to one of the biggest challenges facing the architects — bringing natural light into a massive structure. The light flows down the lightrium's paneled walls, illuminating the law library, the Hughes Memorial Library on the second floor, and the Forum, a spacious and comfortable community assembly area on the first floor. All the spaces are made even cheerier by a color scheme that employs four different shades of golden yellow paint. The darkest shade is used on the first floor, with the shades getting progressively lighter on subsequent floors.

Subtle interior touches — customized furniture by alumnus Daniel Strawn, warm tiles that complement the brick — humanize this sizeable academic space, which might otherwise seem cold and impersonal. Still other amenities connect the program to the larger campus — the black metal stair railings, for example, represent an homage to their counterparts in the Mary Reed Building.

At 242,000 square feet (which includes the parking level in the basement), the Ricketson Law Building includes numerous communal spaces for student-professor interaction. Chief among them is the Forum, the first space to greet visitors as they enter through the main doors. This open-air, two-level meeting space, which doubles as an informal "town hall" venue for outside speakers, was modeled after a facility at Harvard's John F. Kennedy School of Government.

Additional communal spaces include the Robert B. Yegge Commons, named in honor of a longtime faculty

member and former law dean who served from 1965 to 1977. The commons serves as an informal center for coffee, meals, and conversation. On the third and fourth floors, roomy faculty offices are located in pods not too far from student lockers. This positioning was designed to promote interaction, with professors and students meeting in the hallways on their way to and from classes. To the delight of the architects, one professor has taken this design scheme to heart by insisting that all meetings with students occur in the hallway outside his office. In this less hierarchical setting, tension and pressure are dissipated.

Initially, the wide corridors struck some of the law faculty as wasteful and excessive. But Pring believes the benefits far outweigh any detriments. "We did not want the place to look like Alcatraz," he said. "It used to scare me going to other law schools, because I felt like a little kid again, when I would get in those dark hallways seeing nothing but professors closing doors."

Flexible and functional learning spaces are spread throughout the building and further student-faculty inter-action. Designed to reduce, rather than foster, intimidation, the classrooms are painted in warm hues and scaled to

suggest intimacy. The inventory includes ten tiered rooms and four seminar rooms. Rather than provide large, one-size-fits-all classrooms for courses across the specialties, the architects planned for classes of varying sizes. The largest of the tiered classrooms holds 120 students, but other classrooms accommodate ninety, seventy, and fifty students.

Where the Park Hill facility included a seldom-used 500-seat auditorium, the Ricketson Law Building defers to the campus' other resources. Should any event require that much seating, the college can book the Davis Auditorium in nearby Sturm Hall. This way, the law school can take maximum advantage of the university's resources without paying to heat, cool, and maintain an infrequently used auditorium.

The Ricketson Law Building also contains two moot courtrooms where students hone the skills they will need for trial work. The larger of the two courtrooms doubles as a venue for continuing legal education classes, which are mandatory for any Colorado lawyer with an active license. As an added benefit, the Colorado Supreme Court will, on occasion, try cases on campus, providing Sturm College students a firsthand look at the judicial system at work.

ASPHALT CONTROL

As despoilers of beauty and open space, parking lots and garages have few rivals. They are, however, necessary evils.

To mitigate their impact on campus and on the surrounding neighborhoods, the university created strategically located multilevel parking structures that incorporate materials found in the new buildings. For example, the Ricketson Law Building's four-level garage boasts a red brick and limestone exterior that blends in with the building itself. Cranberry light poles, fixtures, and handrails add a DU polish to the structure. Other parking structures are clad in copper or accented in limestone. The Newman Center's garage is tucked discreetly behind the building and accessed through a side street, thus minimizing its visual impact.

In the interests of adding 3,155 new parking spaces while containing each parking structure's footprint, many of the new garages feature underground levels—a costly move deemed essential to preserving green space and views. For example, Nelson Hall's two-level garage, which offers parking to its student residents, is completely below ground. In fact, the residence hall's interior grass courtyard sits directly on top of the parking facility—a pleasing departure from the university's former reliance on sprawling surface lots.

WESTMINSTER LAW LIBRARY

At most law schools, the law library is the nerve center of the program. That's especially true of the Sturm College of Law's Westminster Law Library.

Geoff Freeman, principal of SBRA of Boston, oversaw the design of the Westminster Law Library and knows the role that libraries play in training qualified attorneys. "Today, the square footage of a library is not the primary measure of quality. Instead, the success of the library is determined by its services and the level of scholarship that takes place. A library needs to make connections," Freeman said.

At the Westminster Law Library, connectivity begins at the front doors with a welcoming circulation desk crafted by Strawn. Frequently used materials, including reference collections, are approachable and unintimidating—a pleasing departure from how comparable resources are housed at many other institutions, where, in the words of library director Gary Alexander, these resources appear to be "locked up and inaccessible." On the third floor, students emerging from the internal staircase are immediately greeted by a small, unassuming desk staffed by a qualified librarian who can direct them to the resources they need.

Thanks to sophisticated cataloging technology and the miracles of compact shelving, Freeman was able to craft a design that emphasizes workspace rather than storage space. Most of the 36,000-square-foot library's rare volumes are stored on the first floor, where they are protected but easily accessed. Large panes of glass separate the majority of the library's open space from the rest of the building. The glass stifles any sound emanating from the hallways, and it also makes it possible for students and faculty to peer into and out of the library. Because the glass maximizes the amount of natural light that penetrates the space, very little artificial lighting is needed. The existing light fixtures, like others in the building, are programmed to dim or brighten according to the amount of natural light cast through the windows and lightrium.

The library also affords easy access to breakout rooms for group study. These, too, feature glass walls, enhancing the building's sense of transparency and, again, maximizing the benefits of natural light. Like so many of the building's spaces, the breakout rooms serve to bring people together and make the law school experience more pleasurable.

At Ritchie's urging, the American Bar Association (ABA) relaxed its requirement that law libraries had to have seating capacity for fifty percent of a school's student population.

In DU's case, that would have meant 600 seats within the confines of the library. The ABA agreed to count spaces outside the library but inside the school. As a result, the Westminster Law Library is almost 20,000 square feet smaller than its predecessor on the Park Hill campus, which also housed study rooms, law review offices, computer labs, and storage. At the Ricketson Law Building, those services are scattered throughout the building, thus encouraging collaborative learning and shared experiences.

GOLD AND GLISTENING

The Ricketson Law Building qualified for its LEED gold certification in 2003. Since its opening, the conservation benefits have added up—to name just one indicator, the building uses forty percent less water thanks to various low-flow fixtures and water recycling systems. The building's impact on the Colorado environment was also minimized. For example, an astounding seventy-five percent of all construction waste was recycled, diverting tons of refuse from landfills. What's more, Ritchie encouraged the building committee to insist on using postconsumer, recycled products, so the roof features recycled copper, and the carpeting is made of recycled milk cartons.

Surveying the end result, Pring comes to one conclusion. "No law school should be the first in the twenty-first century *not* to build by these standards," he said.

GREEN QUALITIES

What makes the Ricketson Law Building green? What makes it worthy of a gold certification from the U.S. Green Building Council?

ENERGY CONSERVATION
• efficient electric lighting strategies
• occupancy turn-off sensors
• high-efficiency mechanical systems
• high thermal performance walls
• energy-saving windows and roof
• use of renewable energy including wind

WATER CONSERVATION
• infrared sensors on water faucets
• waterless urinals
• low-flow toilets
• recycling of natural groundwater for landscape irrigation
• a storm water system that reduces and naturally filters runoff

MATERIALS
• recycled structural steel, copper, carpeting, acoustic tile
• preference, when possible, for locally manufactured materials
• durable materials that require less long-term maintenance
• unpainted brick for interior walls, thus reducing the need to paint and re-paint

PROMOTING RECYCLING
• recycling bins for glass, paper, and plastics on every floor
• use of construction materials, like copper, that can be recycled

REDUCED LIGHT POLLUTION
• specially designed exterior lighting

AIR QUALITY
• carbon monoxide monitoring system
• low volatile organic compounds (VOC) paint
• chemical and pollutant controls

AN INNOVATIVE LIGHTRIUM IS CREATED BY A SKYLIGHT THAT FILLS THE CENTER OF THE BUILDING WITH THE SUN'S RAYS, WHICH ARE DISSEMINATED TO OTHER PARTS OF THE BUILDING BY WINDOWS IN THE INTERIOR WALLS. THE DESIGN TEAM DELIBERATELY LINED MANY OF THE WIDE HALLWAYS WITH LOCKERS, SO THAT PROFESSORS "WOULD TRIP OVER STUDENTS ON THEIR WAY TO CLASS," MARK RODGERS SAID. ON THE FACING PAGE, AN INTERNAL STAIRCASE CONNECTS THE VARIOUS FLOORS OF THE WESTMINSTER LAW LIBRARY. ITS LANDINGS PROVIDE AN OPPORTUNITY FOR STUDENTS TO STOP AND GAZE AT THE SKY.

Education at the University of Denver is an active process. Students learn by doing, by putting their classroom knowledge to the test in settings that replicate the workplace conditions they will encounter after graduation. At the School of Hotel, Restaurant, and Tourism Management, students learn the ins and outs of running a hospitality enterprise, while graduate students in education test theories and apply new knowledge at the on-campus Donne and Sue Fisher Early Learning Center. Meanwhile, law students hone their trial skills in the mock courtrooms at the Frank H. Ricketson Jr. Law Building.

LABORATORIES FOR EXPERIENTIAL LEARNING

7

"Yes, but ..."

— MARK RODGERS

THE LEARNING ENVIRONMENT INSIDE THE SCHOOL OF HOTEL, RESTAURANT, AND TOURISM MANAGEMENT BUILDING, SHOWN ON PAGE 152, WAS DESIGNED TO SHARPEN THE PROGRAM'S COMPETITIVE EDGE IN A FIELD CHARACTERIZED BY TOP-NOTCH OFFERINGS. IN THE BUILDING'S BEVERAGE MANAGEMENT CENTER, LEFT, STUDENTS PUT CLASSROOM AND TEXTBOOK LEARNING TO WORK. THAT SAME PHILOSOPHY APPLIES AT THE FISHER EARLY LEARNING CENTER, PICTURED ABOVE, WHERE THE PLAY AND LEARNING SPACES COMPLEMENT THE CURRICULUM.

PRACTICING HOSPITALITY

It was the supreme irony. For too many years, students in the Daniels College of Business' School of Hotel, Restaurant, and Tourism Management (HRTM) took classes in one of the least hospitable settings on campus.

Originally launched in 1946, the program was conducted out of the second and third floors of the now-demolished Columbine Hall, previously an undistinguished apartment building. Although Columbine had been remodeled in the early 1980s

SCHOOL OF HRTM

School of Hotel, Restaurant, and Tourism Management

ARCHITECT OF RECORD
Gensler Architects

CONTRACTOR
The Weitz Company

BUDGET
$17.5 million

SQUARE FOOTAGE
45,000

to add much-needed classroom space, it nonetheless smacked of the makeshift. While functional, the spaces left much to be desired.

Fast forward to 1998, when the chancellor and trustees agreed that the hospitality school needed a facility worthy of the nationally ranked program. In one of his last acts as university architect, Cab Childress attended classes at the school and began creating initial sketches for a three-story building to be sited between the Evans Chapel and the Driscoll Student Center.

While the ink was still drying on Childress' drawings, the project was abruptly put on hold when design and construction priorities shifted, thanks to the unexpectedly quick sale of the Park Hill campus and the pressing need to relocate the Women's College and the law school to University Park. Childress retired soon after that, leaving the fledgling project on the drawing boards. It would fall to Mark Rodgers — whom Childress affectionately described as a "yes, but …" architect — to bring the building to life.

THE RED-TILE DOME ON THE SCHOOL OF HOTEL,
RESTAURANT, AND TOURISM MANAGEMENT
BUILDING IS SEPARATED FROM THE ROOFLINE BY
PANES OF CURVED GLASS THAT BRING SUN- AND
MOONLIGHT INTO THE INTERIOR. THE STRUCTURE
INCORPORATES THE UNIVERSITY'S SIGNATURE
MATERIALS WHILE DRAWING UPON A FAMOUS
TUSCAN ESTATE FOR DESIGN INSPIRATION.

Rodgers earned his "yes, but …" designation because of his habit of greeting all of Childress' pronouncements with a mixture of agreement and contradiction. Rodgers can often see all sides of a story and empathize with all sides of an argument. That talent was to serve him well once work began on the new hospitality school building, whose occupants would be trained to anticipate and satisfy the often contradictory whims of a demanding public.

By 2002, with the law building under construction, HRTM was at the top of Rodgers' list of hot-button projects. His marching orders came from Peter Rainsford, who served as HRTM director from 1999 to 2006. Rainsford came to DU from the School of Hotel Administration at Cornell University and brought with him definite ideas about the type of facility needed to ensure that the DU program remained among the top in the nation.

As Rodgers remembers it, Rainsford gave the architect a number of concepts to keep foremost in his mind. First, HRTM is a management school, in which students are trained to manage resorts, restaurants, country clubs — in fact, the full gamut of hospitality enterprises. And rather than learn how to run, say, just one hotel, students should leave the university understanding how to manage an entire chain of hotels.

With this in mind, Rainsford wanted the new facility to be a "management laboratory," where students combined theory with real-world experience. In Rainsford's vision, students would immerse themselves in the details and the big picture. They would learn to oversee day-to-day operations and coordinate events, everything from private gatherings for dignitaries to wedding receptions. "I want the students to understand what it's like to serve the mother of the bride," Rainsford told Rodgers.

Joined by Gensler Architects, the architect of record, Rodgers and Rainsford pursued a design that reflected the sophisticated hospitality found in Old World Europe, where the art of service has been refined over hundreds of years. Their primary inspiration was the well-known Banfi Estate in Italy, which is highly respected for its vineyards and hostelry.

The fruit of this collaboration incorporates a palette of red brick, granite, limestone, and copper — materials that integrate effortlessly with nearby Nelson and Nagel Halls. The building also features a prominent dome clad in glazed red tile and accented with gold leaf. Its construction was no easy feat, as each ring of tile became progressively smaller.

Rodgers originally suggested that the dome should be anchored by a series of prominent stone columns, but

Rainsford felt that it should appear to float above the rest of the structure like a parachute. In classic "yes, but …" mode, Rodgers agreed, but pushed the idea even further, arguing that the connection between dome and building should be as imperceptible as possible. To that end, the final design enlisted curved panes of glass to separate the dome from the structure. The glass allowed for rays of sun- and moonlight to flood the building. Finally, the bright red tile positions the building among a host of copper- and gold-topped towers, giving it a distinctive signature and making it a campus landmark.

BIENVENIDOS, WILKOMMEN, WELCOME

A hospitality school/management laboratory should, at the very least, invite and welcome. It should set — and meet — high standards.

And nothing says welcome quite like a pineapple — long a widely recognized symbol of generous hospitality. Just above the exterior front door, a bas relief representation of the tropical fruit signals the building's purpose and beckons passersby to venture inside, where the program's high standards are immediately communicated in the high-ceilinged foyer. Flooded by natural light, the three-story rotunda reminds visitors that presentation is, if not everything, certainly important.

The lessons continue throughout the 45,000-square-foot building. The first floor, or garden level, features a 120-person dining hall with an adjacent patio — the perfect setting for an office party or a wedding reception. (With the Evans Chapel next door, the dining hall and patio have become a natural site for postnuptial events.) The dining hall is accessed from the rotunda by a formal staircase crafted for grand entrances. When designing it, Rodgers envisioned a white-garbed bride descending into a waiting crowd of well-wishers.

The dining area is serviced by a 2,800-square-foot full-production kitchen, where students prepare and oversee the service of everything from hors d'oeuvres to desserts. A beverage management center, modeled after a Tuscan wine cellar, allows students to learn about the evaluation and service of fine vintages. Down the hall, an amphitheater-style classroom has distance-learning capabilities, meaning students can benefit from demonstrations conducted on the other side of the continent.

The second floor doubles as the lobby level and features

a hotel front desk, concierge areas, and a business center. It also includes meeting and seminar rooms, as well as breakout rooms for group study. The top floor is home to faculty and staff offices, a student-faculty commons, a high-tech boardroom, and additional breakout rooms. The space was originally intended to house three model hotel guest rooms, but it is also suitable for other uses.

Within this building, students learn according to a philosophy that immerses them in every aspect of the hospitality business. Borrowing from the Daniels College of Business internship program, which maintains that students should learn what it is like to work in the mailroom as well as the boardroom, the School of Hotel, Restaurant, and Tourism Management educates students about all facets of the hospitality business. They learn how to prepare and present high-quality food, how to store and serve fine beverages, how to sell and market events, how to keep the books, and how to evaluate operations to ensure success.

According to David Corsun, current director of the school, the building allows the program to emphasize specialization in, say, restaurant operations or food and beverage management. Such specialization, he said, is in high demand by the industry. The space is also flexible, meaning Corsun can introduce new operations that provide training for an ever-changing industry. For example, the school is planning a full-service, student-run coffee bar in part of the restaurant space. This feature will be a useful asset for students marketing the building's conference and meeting facilities.

"Our goal is to train students to become lifelong learners with strong moral compasses, great communication skills, self-knowledge, and an understanding about how to run a business," Corsun said. The building makes that all the easier.

THE DINING ROOM ACCOMMODATES UP TO 120 PEOPLE COMFORTABLY. IT OPENS TO A SHELTERED PATIO EMBRACED BY A ROCK WALL.

INSIDE THE LIGHT-FILLED ROTUNDA, BALCONIES
AND ARCHES CALL AN ITALIAN VILLA TO MIND.
THE BUILDING'S DESIGN WAS HEAVILY
INFLUENCED BY THE WARM AND WELCOMING
CULTURE OF OLD WORLD EUROPE.

THE CURRICULUM AT THE SCHOOL OF HOTEL, RESTAURANT, AND TOURISM MANAGEMENT IMMERSES STUDENTS IN THE DETAILS AND THE BIG-PICTURE ASPECTS OF THE HOSPITALITY INDUSTRY. THE NEW BUILDING PROVIDES A MANAGEMENT LABORATORY IN WHICH STUDENTS CAN OVERSEE EVERY ASPECT OF THE OPERATIONS, FROM FOOD AND BEVERAGE SERVICE TO EVENT MARKETING AND OPERATIONS MANAGEMENT.

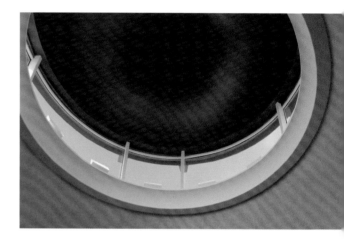

MARK RODGERS

curiosity. It wasn't unusual for Rodgers to find his father seated in a chair with a newspaper in front of him, a short-wave radio tuned to the BBC, the television broadcasting *Meet the Press*, and a nearby computer challenging him to a chess match. "I grew up in a house where there wasn't a wall that wasn't filled with books," he said, describing his father's periodic trips to bookstores that yielded boxes of new volumes.

Rodgers' career ambitions were nearly thwarted when he arrived at Bowdoin College in Maine for the first day of classes. He intended to study architecture, but discovered, too late, that the institution had not offered any architecture classes in years. Although architecture classes were listed in the course-offerings manual, the listings were accompanied by a small symbol designating them as dormant.

"At some point in Bowdoin's 200-year history, there had been an architecture program," Rodgers said. "I never bothered to figure out that the little symbol meant that it wasn't being offered currently."

Despite the setback, Rodgers was undeterred. He majored in physics and art, with a minor in history. Along with several classmates, he convinced Bowdoin's administration to re-institute some architecture classes. In 1988, with his undergraduate degree in hand, Rodgers enrolled in graduate studies at the University of Pennsylvania.

When Mark Rodgers was a precocious three-year-old, he built a hotel out of Legos.

At Penn, Rodgers met his future wife, Valerie Hutchison, an architecture student from Denver. When he began his job hunt, he decided he would like to move west, the better to continue the courtship. He wrote to Hutchison and asked about job prospects in her hometown. She sent him a list of firms with notes about each. At the top of the list, she named G. Cabell Childress Architects. Her accompanying note was loaded with unintended irony: "Best designer in Colorado. Really small office. You don't have a chance."

His grandmother, visiting at the time, asked him if he planned to be an architect when he grew up. "I said, 'What's an architect?'" Rodgers recalled. On hearing her answer, his response was certain. "Then I am going to be an architect."

Born in New Bedford, Massachusetts, in 1965, Rodgers grew up in a Navy family, moving to a different city each time his father was assigned to a new base or ship. Over the years, he could remember the various postings by the roofs that were characteristic of the architecture.

Undeterred again, Rodgers sent a letter to Childress, as well as eleven missives to other Denver firms. He heard from only one.

From these frequent moves, he acquired a taste for adventure. From his mother, who believed fiercely in the value of education, he learned to prize learning opportunities. And from his father—captain of the USS Henry B. Wilson and a key player in the 1975 rescue of a U.S. container ship seized by the Khmer Rouge—Rodgers inherited an insatiable

Rodgers' first meeting with Childress took place in the latter's downtown Denver offices at 1433 Market Street. Rodgers had brought a portfolio of drawings, and after scanning them quickly, Childress closed the book and asked his standard question: Where have you been?

Rodgers had, like Childress, been hither and yon. Over the course of the next few hours, the two shared a long-ranging conversation about place, about the Navy, about how the night lights in mountain towns call to mind the view from a ship as it approaches land. They also talked about why buildings are built where they are, why and how people use them, and how buildings change over time. As they chatted, the day waned, and the office shut down around them.

That was the beginning of a rewarding fourteen-year collaboration characterized by a shared appreciation for philosophical musings, as well as an unrelenting urge to learn and understand. "We just connected," Childress recalled, noting that the two of them shared a mysterious chemistry. "When it's there, you sort of know it. ... Mark knows what it is to have a curiosity."

Rodgers also connected with Dan Ritchie, whose ethic of responsibility reminded the architect of his father. "It was always clear that excuses didn't mean much to Dan. Solutions mattered," Rodgers said, recounting his day-to-day working relationship with Ritchie. Ritchie also taught him much about the value of bold vision. "Dan was not concerned with popular perception. He was interested in creating by taking forward steps. And not baby steps, but strides. You knew you could trust him not to waver."

Rodgers became university architect in 1999, after Childress retired. Since then, he has left his own mark on the university campus while doing his best to reinforce Childress' legacy. "I learned a great deal from Cab," Rodgers said. "He spent a lot of years acquiring knowledge in other places around the world. It has taught me to step back and value certain architectural aspects, as well as how to assess what is in store for the future."

Another thing Rodgers learned from Childress was the value of collaborating with the client, with every occupant of a building. In all of his work for DU, Rodgers has sought to learn from the faculty and professionals destined to work in his buildings, spending hours listening to them describe how they teach and how students learn. He has converted this knowledge into ideal environments for faculty-student exchange.

Reviewing his work at DU, Rodgers counts himself lucky to have been on the ground floor of a project that harnessed his vast and varied enthusiasms and that drew upon his life experiences. "During the summer of 1990," he said, "I spent six weeks in Japan through a study-away program of Penn's. I returned broke, credit cards maxed out, only enough change in my pockets for the subway fare back into Philadelphia and back to Valerie. It was the richest moment of my life. The commitment in Japanese architecture to tradition tangled up with the modern really prepared me to embrace Cab's dismissal of 'style.' ... I think the great styles don't ever start as a style, but rather begin as a commitment to some fundamental visceral attachment to an ideal that, as it becomes recognized, is eventually labeled a style. In effect, because the work here is now commonly called a 'DU style,' it could only be that way because we didn't start with the ideal of a style in the first place."

Today, Rodgers' work advances his appreciation for tradition and innovation—two characteristics especially valuable in a campus environment. Although most of the new buildings on campus benefit from his contributions, he can claim full credit for, among others, the King Lee and Shirley Nelson Residence Hall, the building housing the School of Hotel, Restaurant, and Tourism Management, and the Donne and Sue Fisher Early Learning Center.

Each of these buildings shows Rodgers' passion for inter-connecting influences and his ethic for restraint. "Cab would say that at some point, you have to stop throwing all good ideas into a current project and save them for another design, because the present work will become too cluttered and lose its simplicity," Rodgers said.

As university architect, Rodgers preaches collaboration among all parties in the design and construction process. His years at DU have taught him that there are rarely any "right" answers when it comes to architectural design. Rather, he said, good architecture evolves, "just like a living organism."

A LEARNING LABORATORY FOR EARLY CHILDHOOD EDUCATION

As education professor Toni Linder remembers it, talk about an on-campus early childhood education center first surfaced at DU in the early 1970s. Along with some of her colleagues at the College of Education, Linder envisioned a center that would employ the best practices in the field and that would give education students the chance to deploy and develop their knowledge in a learning laboratory and research center.

FISHER EARLY LEARNING

**Donne and Sue Fisher
Early Learning Center**

ARCHITECT OF RECORD
Andrews & Anderson Architects

CONTRACTOR
Etkin Skanska

BUDGET
$4 million

SQUARE FOOTAGE
18,000

For two decades, the talk continued. "Nothing really happened until Dan Ritchie became chancellor," Linder said. At that point, the early learning center was put on the construction wish list—both as an academic building and as a convenient, reliable education option for university faculty and staff. "Our mission," Linder said, "was to develop a program that would make a contribution to the community and be a place where we could really showcase what optimal childcare looked like and was about." The only way to achieve this goal was to develop a curriculum *and* a building that complemented one another.

With lead donations in hand from Ritchie and Donne and Sue Fisher, the design of the building fell to Rodgers, who had helped Childress with an addition to the Ricks Center for Gifted Children, also housed on the university campus. That project introduced him to the concept of spaces specially designed to support a curriculum and an educational philosophy. That said, the early childhood center assumed additional importance for Rodgers when the phone rang one day in 1996. Rodgers remembers the call well. It came on October 14, the day before his first child was born. The caller was conducting a survey. Did Rodgers have a child and any need for an on-campus source of childhood education? "Well, not yet," he answered. "But tomorrow I'm supposed to."

On a February morning in 1998, after a crash course in all things related to state-of-the-art early learning, Rodgers was scheduled to present his drawings for the proposed center to the university's building and grounds committee. His presentation was forestalled by sudden news: His wife had gone into labor with their second child. In the best show-must-go-on tradition, he handed his designs to Ritchie with a note: "We need to have this facility—now!"

READ, PLAY, AND LEARN!

Rodgers was not alone in his urgency. From the time ground broke on the Donne and Sue Fisher Early Learning Center until its opening, DU employees and parents from throughout the city clamored for spots for their children. The need for a quality center, particularly one linked to a highly respected education program, proved substantial. So substantial, in fact, that by the time the center opened, it was maintaining a growing waiting list.

Marcee Martin, executive director of the center, believes that curriculum-supported programs can make a critical difference in a child's development. "Children live their lives and test out what life is about through stories," she said. That concept underpins the Fisher Center's curriculum, Read, Play, and Learn!

The center's educational foundation—based on research about how children learn, develop, and play—emphasizes an interdisciplinary approach to emerging literacy skill development. A series of instructional teaching modules, created by Linder and customized by each faculty member, helps develop vocabulary, thinking, sequencing, and problem-solving skills through imaginative play—whether a child has special needs, is at risk, or is developmentally challenged.

In the interests of increasing the university's outreach to the community and disseminating the center's educational philosophy throughout the region, the center's bylaws stipulate that forty percent of the facility's 190-plus students come from the Denver community at large. Sixty percent of the slots are reserved for the children of DU faculty and staff. Ritchie and Linder hoped that by introducing the larger community to a high-quality, education-focused facility, they would increase the demand for comparable

THE EXTERIOR DESIGN OF THE FISHER EARLY LEARNING CENTER, PAGE 168, PLAYFULLY SUGGESTS A RAILWAY STATION. INSIDE, CLASSROOM SPACES ACCOMMODATE THE MANY ACTIVITIES SUPPORTED BY THE READ, PLAY, AND LEARN! CURRICULUM.

WHEN DESIGNING THE FISHER EARLY LEARNING
CENTER, RODGERS SOUGHT TO AVOID THE
INSTITUTIONAL LOOK OF MANY EDUCATION
FACILITIES. THE DOORS AND FIXTURES ARE SIZED
WITH TODDLERS IN MIND, AND MOST OF THE
CLASSROOMS HAVE CUSHIONS AND SOFT
SURFACES TO ACCOMMODATE ROBUST PLAY.
IN ADDITION, CLASSROOMS OPEN TO THE
OUTDOORS, WHICH KEEPS CHILDREN FROM
FEELING CONFINED.

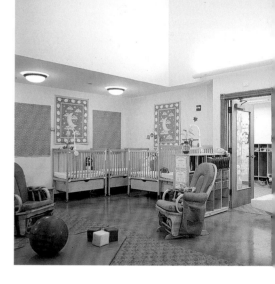

THE RECEPTION AREA SETS THE TONE FOR THE REST OF THE BUILDING, WHICH INCORPORATES NATURAL COLORS AND MATERIALS. ACTING ON THE ADVICE OF DU'S EDUCATION FACULTY, THE DESIGN TEAM CREATED AN ENVIRONMENT THAT OFFERED JUST THE RIGHT MIX OF SENSORY STIMULATION. TOO MUCH CAN PROVE CONFUSING AND DISORIENTING; TOO LITTLE CAN MAKE A SPACE UNWELCOMING AND FORBIDDING.

programs. "Dan wanted Fisher to be a catalyst for the community," Linder said. "We also wanted a diverse population, and that is something we really worked to get in this facility."

The center is staffed by a team of forty, including teachers, educators, and administrators, as well as the Fisher Inclusion Team (FIT). This specialized group consists of occupational therapists, speech therapists, music therapists, social workers, and early childhood special educators. Their role is to assist children in need of a little extra attention. Morgridge College of Education graduate students also get the opportunity to witness, via closed-circuit television in a second-floor conference room, what Linder calls "trans-disciplinary play-based assessment"—an assessment of a child that involves professional team members and family members. The session takes place in one of the center's multipurpose rooms, a welcoming space full of toys, games, and books.

All of this work is enhanced by Rodgers' handiwork and the contributions of Andrews & Anderson, the architect of record. Together, they crafted a building that allows graduate students to conduct research on early child development, that reinforces a curriculum rooted in best practices, and that provides children a pleasant and stimulating setting for play and learning.

Located at the prime western entry to the campus, the 18,000-square-foot building carefully blends in with nearby residences. Its exterior was designed to foster a smooth transition from a quiet neighborhood into the heart of campus. The building's red brick, limestone trim, and copper roof let passersby know that it belongs to campus. Meanwhile, to ensure that the building does not dominate its neighbors, its scale reflects the one- and two-story houses nearby. DU purchased a small brick bungalow to the north of the center and then connected the two buildings with a brick-enclosed thoroughfare and a ramp. Among other amenities, the bungalow features a child-friendly library and sitting area, as well as full-service kitchen. "We always intended to leave the building there as sort of the university's transition back to the community," Linder said.

Rodgers' personal touches are evident throughout the Fisher Center, where two of his three children embarked on their education odyssey. To give the building a soothing appearance, and to make it seem a safe and welcoming place for toddlers and tykes, Rodgers had the red brick tumbled extensively to create smooth edges and corners. A limestone sill and copper-trimmed "eyebrow" window give the front

a touch of whimsy, while inside the front doors, two side-by-side entryways—one sized for parents and one sized just for toddlers and preschoolers—lead into the building. A domed ceiling painted with blue sky and clouds draws children down the hallway to their classrooms. Throughout the center, lower ceilings and lower windows, lockers, sinks, and toilets cater to the building's chief tenants. "We set the scale so the kids feel it is meant mostly for them," Rodgers explained.

Each of the eleven sound-reducing classrooms is named after a major children's storybook. The rooms are brightened by abundant sunlight and walls painted in natural-toned colors. To encourage exuberant play, the floors have padded matting. Each classroom has curriculum-specific spaces designed to be re-arranged every two to three weeks, as well as ample space for science experimentation. A partnership between the Fisher Center and the University of Denver Lamont School of Music brings music students to the building for demonstrations and performances, so it's not uncommon for the sounds of saxophones and clarinets, for the strains of Beethoven and the beat of marching drums to fill the rooms.

Upstairs, on the second floor, an observation area encourages parents, graduate students, and administrators to observe the action in the classrooms below. During lunch hours, it is not uncommon to find DU parents peering through the windows, watching their children interact with peers or tackle a puzzle.

A spacious padded-floor "motor room," located just off the school's playgrounds, gives children room to romp when bad weather brings them inside. It doubles as an auditorium for dramatic play and as a training site for educators from around the community who share in-service training.

"The building enables spaces to be used in many ways," Linder said. "The space flows from inside to outside, from room to room, and into the halls. Staff and children use every inch of space. … And, of course, the children love the tiny child-sized doors."

COURT
IS IN SESSION

Nothing prepares an attorney for the courtroom quite like experience.

That's why the Frank H. Ricketson Jr. Law Building includes two moot courtrooms where Sturm College of Law students can question witnesses, present arguments, contend with the rulings of judges, and experience firsthand the intricacies of the justice system.

The courtrooms provide the backdrop for the Student Trial Lawyers Association's annual intramural mock trial program, where teams of first-year students are assigned a problem that must be resolved before the bench. Teams are coached by second- and third-year law students, who help strategize case theories, draft opening and closing statements, and develop direct and cross examinations. The teams then participate in three mock trial rounds against other teams, with the first round judged by advanced law students, the second by practicing trial attorneys, and the third by experienced judges. With each round, students learn about how best to represent their clients in the courtroom.

Students can also observe the system in action. On occasion, the Colorado Supreme Court will review a case in the larger of the two courtrooms, whose walls and seating can be reconfigured to accommodate up to 120 people.

The moot courtrooms incorporate amenities found in state-of-the-art facilities across the country. In addition to the standard witness stand, judge's bench, and prosecution and defense tables, the courtrooms feature the latest in video recording capabilities and projection screens—which can be used for analyzing mock jury deliberations. The hand-carved appellate bench, created by local furniture designers Daniel and Karen Strawn, gives students a sense of what it is like to take a case through the appeals process, where a panel of judges reviews procedures and issues rulings.

Whether small and discreet or super-sized and prominent, the art commissioned for the University of Denver's new buildings was tasked with a big job: to elevate, rather than simply accent, the architecture. The result is a seamless blend of art and setting, of expression and storytelling.

A MARRIAGE OF ART AND ARCHITECTURE

8

"Buildings that people smile about tend to be the ones that people want to take care of."

— MARK RODGERS

INSIDE THE RITCHIE CENTER'S WILLIAMS TOWER, PICTURED ON PAGE 176, TROMPE L'OEIL ARTISTS CONVERTED ONCE-WHITE WALLS INTO A VISUAL EXTRAVAGANZA. THE RITCHIE CENTER'S EL POMAR NATATORIUM IS HOME TO A TILE MURAL, SHOWN ABOVE, BY MAYNARD TISCHLER OF THE SCHOOL OF ART AND ART HISTORY. ANOTHER FACULTY MEMBER, LAWRENCE ARGENT, ADDED TO THE CAMPUS' ART COLLECTION WITH WHISPERS, AN INTERACTIVE INSTALLATION THAT UTILIZES AUDIOTAPES TO START A CONVERSATION.

At its best, art can challenge assumptions, stimulate thought, and evoke powerful emotions. It can also work with the architecture around it to tell a story and to cultivate enduring affection for a place or a building.

When commissioning art for the various buildings on campus, Dan Ritchie, Cab Childress, and the numerous architects involved departed from the art-as-afterthought practices common to many large-scale design projects. "Art on our campus is not just a bust, or a painting in a building, or an outdoor sculpture. As much as it is about the art, it is also about its location, how it fits, and whether or not its value transcends its architecture encasement," explained Mark Rodgers, noting that each commission was subjected to a simple but exacting test: "Does it make the architecture better? And does the architecture make the sculpture successful?"

In other words, does the art feel as much a part of the building as its front door and windows? Would the building seem diminished without it? Does it generate a smile?

As if that were not challenge enough, the new art also needed to coexist peacefully with the university's existing inventory, which included a handful of landmark installations much loved by alumni. Among these was the *Alma Mater* sculpture, with its two women poring over an open book. Originally positioned just outside Margery Reed Mayo Hall and presented to the university by Mrs. Verner Z. Reed, in memory of her daughter and the building's namesake, the sculpture was later relocated to the Harper Humanities Gardens. The green space begged for a focal point, and the *Alma Mater* statue provided a poetic accent. What's more, its initial position in front of Margery Reed Mayo Hall was undoubtedly cumbersome, an impediment to graduation ceremonies and other events scheduled on the green.

THE ALMA MATER *STATUE, BELOW, ORIGINALLY STOOD OUTSIDE MARGERY REED MAYO HALL. IT WAS LATER MOVED TO THE HARPER HUMANITIES GARDENS. CHARLES O. PERRY'S* POETRY IN STEEL, *PAGE 179, ONCE FILLED THE SPACE BETWEEN UNIVERSITY HALL AND THE MARY REED BUILDING. IT WAS LATER POSITIONED NEAR THE ENTRANCE TO PENROSE LIBRARY, WHERE IT STANDS TODAY.*

Still another existing piece, the elegant *Poetry in Steel* by Charles O. Perry, sits outside Penrose Library. It calls attention to the library's entrance, but is otherwise unrelated to the building. "That would not happen today at DU because we're more than just a sculpture gallery," Rodgers said.

In planning the art for each building, Childress and Rodgers strove for harmony, where possible incorporating each installation into the early drawings. Before the foundation was laid on any given building, the contractor was shown where much of the artwork would be positioned. To Rodgers' mind, this approach was akin to buying a sculpted building and campus. "The buildings at DU are at their best because they are located at the University of Denver and nowhere else. I think that is something that holds true for the art as well," he said.

Childress, for his part, was careful about just how much art to incorporate in a building. The relationship between art and architecture, he believed, should evolve throughout the building's lifespan. "You don't want to finish a building, you want to start it," Childress often said, noting that art should be added by each generation of users. The architect's responsibility is to create a backdrop for future creativity, whether it is the addition of a favorite postcard collection to an office wall or the inclusion of a sculpture in a niche. That said, he also believed that the initial art should set a standard for the art to come.

To start the centuries-long creative process, Childress relied on a stable of artists and craftsmen with whom he had worked for years. Believing that art should reflect the enthusiasms of the building's owners, he also called on Ritchie to bring big-picture perspective and aesthetic preferences to the collaborative team. And then, he let the creative process take its course. "All I'm doing," he said, "is encouraging the angels."

CHARTING THE EVOLUTION OF COMMUNICATION

A trip inside the Ritchie Center's Williams Tower offers both a visual feast and an informal course in communications history.

The tower is the canvas for four *trompe l'oeil* murals, each depicting a critical stage in the development of human communications. The dawn of communication begins on the east wall with *The Spoken Word*, in which a robed African storyteller is shown sharing a tale with a rapt young listener. The history continues on the north wall, where *The Written Word* features a pharaoh dictating to a scribe. The mural also incorporates ancient alphabets and carvings from the Rosetta stone.

The third mural, titled *The Printed Word*, shows craftsmen working at a printing press. The press is framed by the text of the First Amendment to the U.S. Constitution, reminding viewers about the role a free press has played in our culture. The final mural, which anchors the western wall, conveys the information explosion associated with the *Digital Transformation*. The mural puts Sophia, the goddess of wisdom, at the archway of a new millennium. Waves of DNA and binary code stream from her outstretched hands, while over her head, a sailing Sputnik passes through a sky of stars.

Funded by honorary life trustee Carl Williams and trustee Scott Reiman, the mural was the work of artists Ken Miller and Linda Paulsen, whose firm, Grammar of Ornament, took on the challenge of adorning the 62-foot-high walls. Miller and Paulsen were joined in the project by Karin Mirick and her company, Create-A-Scene.

The mural is a must-see experience for first-year students. Every fall, when the chancellor hosts dinners for newcomers to the campus, first-year students are invited to climb to the top of the tower and play the carillon, if only for a note or two. Along the way, they savor the fruits of human genius.

THE FOUR WALLS INSIDE THE
WILLIAMS TOWER FEATURE A MURAL
THAT CHARTS THE HISTORY OF
COMMUNICATION, BEGINNING WITH
THE SPOKEN WORD AND CULMINATING
WITH THE LIGHTNING-FAST WORLD
OF DIGITAL TECHNOLOGY.

ART INSTALLATIONS ON THE EXTERIOR OF THE NEWMAN CENTER UTILIZE THE BUILDING'S MATERIALS. A SUNDIAL ON THE STRUCTURE'S SOUTH SIDE TELLS TIME IN LIMESTONE. THE BUILDING'S NORTH SIDE, WHICH HOSTS THE ENTRANCE TO TREVORROW HALL, HOME OF THE LAMONT SCHOOL OF MUSIC, IS MARKED BY TWO BAS RELIEF SCULPTURES THAT DEPICT CLASSICAL AND JAZZ MUSICIANS AT WORK. ON THE BUILDING'S WEST SIDE, WHERE PATRONS APPROACH THE VENUE DEDICATED TO THEATER, A LIMESTONE SCULPTURE INTRODUCES CHARACTERS REMINISCENT OF THE COMMEDIA DELL'ARTE.

THE INSIDE STORIES — TOLD IN LIMESTONE

On any walk across campus or stroll through the buildings, the attentive pedestrian will be treated to an unfolding story — relayed in stone and punctuated with humor.

Childress' own playful sense of humor is on display on the north archway outside F.W. Olin Hall, where a small limestone relief identifies the year of construction and depicts two figures bearing the weight of the building's dome on their shoulders. The figures are faceless, but they represent Rodgers and Mike Haden of Soderberg Masonry, two key members of the team that brought Olin Hall to life. Rodgers had put together the architectural layout to the dome and drew many of the limestone pieces, while Haden was the lead mason. The sculpture not only references their role in constructing the dome, it was also a way for Childress to celebrate the collaborative efforts of his team.

Limestone reliefs also serve to identify — with a wink and a nod — a building's purpose. For example, the east and west entrances to the School of Hotel, Restaurant, and Tourism Management are each topped by a limestone pineapple, a widely recognized symbol of hospitality. Centuries ago, the exotic fruit was regarded as the crown jewel of a festive repast, its presence at a banquet providing both visual and culinary delight. Inside the school, of course, students learn about everything the pineapple represents, from the importance of presentation to the pleasures of a warm welcome.

At the Daniels College of Business, a number of exterior limestone reliefs, funded by DU trustee Scott Reiman, president of Hexagon Investments, testify to the pursuits inside the building. Limestone carvings of a bull and bear, recognizable symbols of stock market performance, grace the exterior and represent the study of finance. The building's architect of record, Anderson Mason Dale, incorporated a subtle commerce motif into the building's water table trim, a custom-cut limestone "wrap" around the building's exterior. Upon close scrutiny, a dollar-shaped design reveals itself, symbolizing the role business and commerce play in the creation of wealth. As a tip of the hat to Reiman, Margie Soo Hoo Lee of Childress' campus studio added the limestone grapevine that punctuates the exterior trim. It features tiny hexagon-shaped grapes, a nod to the investment company's logo.

Whimsical statements like these do much more than enhance the visual appeal of the building. They offer stories that can be handed down from one generation to the next. They make the building a fixture in the memory, a site worth loving and preserving.

LIMESTONE RELIEFS, LIKE THESE ON THE EXTERIOR OF OLIN HALL, ARE DESIGNED TO ENGAGE AND ENTERTAIN PASSERSBY.

183

ART AND ARCHITECTURE: TWO-PART HARMONY AT THE NEWMAN CENTER

A building dedicated to the performing arts deserves ovation-worthy visual art.

That is, in part, why Childress' designs for the Robert and Judi Newman Center for the Performing Arts called for two bookend bas reliefs on the building's north entrance. To conjure the right mix of wit and whimsy, he and protégé Keith Connor recommended renowned Colorado sculptors Madeline Wiener and Kathi Caricof.

Both Wiener and Caricof brought years of experience and creativity to the project. Wiener, founder and director of the Marble Institute of Colorado, has been sculpting private and public indoor and outdoor art for the better part of four decades. Her works grace museums, galleries, and private collections all across the globe, from Chicago to Edinburgh, Scotland, and Hyderabad, India.

Caricof's extensive experience is just as impressive. With a background in industrial, graphic, and interior design, and with a passion for sculpting in stone, steel, and glass, Caricof has often joined Wiener on large-scale projects that call for technical precision and creative vision.

The two do much of their work out of the Purple Door Studios, a stone-carving oasis that Wiener launched in Denver's River North arts district. During summers, they transition to a studio in Marble, Colorado, where they host sculptors from all over the world at the annual Marble/marble Symposium. While Wiener and Caricof each have their own independent client base, they enjoy pooling their talents for imaginative endeavors like the DU project.

Wiener and Caricof took on the DU challenge with minimal direction from the institution. The architecture team asked only that the final piece represent a wide range of performers. "Cab Childress had drawn a little sketch that was quite whimsical in nature, so that was what Kathi and I worked off of," Wiener remembered. Together, their two 75,000-pound reliefs, titled *The Spirit of Music*, depict the diverse music-making endeavors inside the building. Each twenty-four-foot-tall relief is cast in a sweeping S-curve that parrots the treble clef. On the east side of the exterior, the relief portrays a jazz combo at work, complete with a saxophone player and a bassist. This relief is located directly over the building's jazz rehearsal studio. The west-end relief pays homage to vocal and instrumental classical music, featuring operatic singers, a violinist, and a trumpeter. Behind that wall, students make full use of the voice studio.

To make their sculptures as lifelike as possible, Wiener and Caricof observed musicians at play. For example, they called on Joe Docksey, director of the Lamont School of

KATHI CARICOF AND MADELINE WIENER, SHOWN
FROM LEFT TO RIGHT IN THE PHOTOGRAPH ON
PAGE 184, MESHED THEIR ARTISTIC AND WORK
STYLES TO COMPLETE THE LIMESTONE BAS RELIEF
SCULPTURE THAT GRACES THE CHAMBERS
CENTER'S GARDEN. THE CENTER IS ALSO HOME
TO MOTHERS' WINDOW, SHOWN BELOW, AN ART
GLASS INSTALLATION COMMISSIONED BY
MICHELLE "MIKE" BLOOM AND HER HUSBAND,
STEVE, TO HONOR THEIR MOTHERS. THE OVAL
WINDOW INCORPORATES EMBEDDED ELEMENTS,
PICTURED AT BOTTOM RIGHT, THAT REFLECT
THE RICHNESS OF WOMEN'S LIVES. A COPPER
MEDALLION BY ARTIST SHARON ANHORN MARKS
THE ENTRANCE TO THE CHAMBERS CENTER.

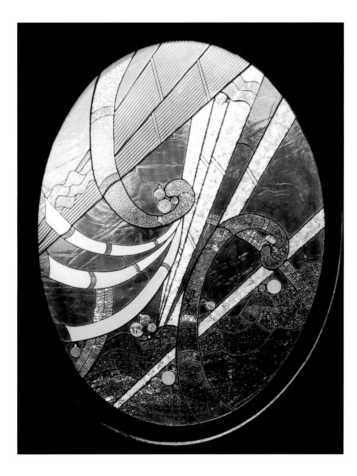

185

Music, to play the trumpet for them so they could replicate the cheeks of a virtuoso in action. "We thoroughly researched orchestras, musicians, and instruments for gestures and overall placement," Wiener said, noting that each detail was honed meticulously to ensure a realistic depiction.

According to Wiener, the two stone reliefs presented a formidable logistics challenge and necessitated renting additional space next to the Purple Door. Much of the work was completed at the Purple Door, but finishing touches were added after the installation in winter 2002. Contending with bitter temperatures and perched on scaffolds forty feet above terra firma—where, should tools fall to the ground, they could not be easily retrieved—Wiener and Caricof worked to join lines and ensure that the final assembly appeared seamless. Because the four six-foot panels had never been stacked on top of each other in the studio, Wiener and Caricof were worried that the panels might not align perfectly. Fortunately, all matched up well, requiring only minor adjustments.

Another potential obstacle—clashing artistic egos—was averted when both women adopted what Wiener calls "a mutually acceptable style that did not show one's strength over the other." In fact, she said, the two agreed to make the final product look like the work of one person. "We had a common goal of making the reliefs look as magnificent as we could."

Wiener and Caricof also collaborated on a limestone installation, titled *Renaissance Chair*, at the Newman Center's west entrance, where arts patrons approach the Byron Flexible Theater, home to DU dramatic productions. This installation showcases Renaissance actors playing out a story of young love and parental disapproval. "Kathi and I wanted to express with this work that the viewer would soon enter a beautiful theater and be ushered to their seat for a trip through the world of the creative. The throne in our sculpture welcomes anyone to sit down before, during, or after the journey. We wanted it to be grand—like the seating feels inside," Wiener said.

The Newman Center's south exterior wall sports a sundial, the brainchild of the team at Anderson Mason Dale, led by architect Andy Nielsen. According to Nielsen, it was meant to be an "artistic icon of the building" and, because sundials are notoriously inaccurate timekeepers, to show the "passage of time and not the telling of time."

The sundial also made clever use of the materials on hand for construction—sun-loving limestone and sun-suggestive Hansen sandstone. Because the sundial is placed on the top half of the building, the gnomon, the triangular metal point that creates the sundial's shadow, is easily visible to passing drivers, allowing them to register the time as they head to their destination. Like most sundials, this one indicates apparent solar time. It cannot be adjusted for daylight savings time, but it is accurate every day at "high noon," a particularly Western touchstone.

A ROSE WINDOW FOR A CATHEDRAL TO ART

Upon returning from a 1999 vacation to France, where he tromped through a host of famous cathedrals, Childress gave Rodgers a marching order. "We need a rose window for the Newman Center," he said. But unlike ecclesiastical rose windows, this one needed to look like a real flower. This rose window, he maintained, should call to mind the roses given a star at performance's end, the traditional way of punctuating a series of bravos.

Intrigued by the idea, Rodgers began looking at roses with fresh eyes. At the Leo Block Alumni Center on the north side of campus, he picked a rose from the garden that greets former students returning to campus for a visit. Rodgers used the shapely specimen to begin his first drawings of the Newman Center's rose window. The final drawings featured a labyrinth of petals. "I wanted people in the building to feel like they were a bee on one of the rose's petals," Rodgers said.

Creating a rose on paper was one thing. Shaping one out of a massive slab of limestone was quite another matter. That challenge fell to Soderberg Masonry's Chuck Nacos, who, like Childress, had traveled extensively in Europe and had developed a reverence for the craftsmanship on display in cathedrals. When Nacos learned about the rose assignment, he submitted a bid that dramatically undercut the competition. Initial estimates were in the range of $200,000, Rodgers recalled, noting that the high costs put the window in jeopardy. Nacos, however, offered to create the window for a mere $6,800—despite the fact that he couldn't be precisely sure how to begin, much less complete, the work. "To be honest with you, we didn't have a clue how to do this window," he said.

But the challenge was part of the charm. "I bid this job because I wanted this rose," Nacos said. "No one will ever do a nicer window."

Today, with its soft edges and subtle curves, the window opens to the west, offering a bee's eye view from the top-floor

MAYNARD TISCHLER'S
SEASCAPES

When ceramicist Maynard Tischler retired from the University of Denver School of Art and Art History in 2008 after forty-two years of service, he left behind a legacy of provocative work and inspired teaching. He also left a tangible display of his creativity inside the Ritchie Center's El Pomar Natatorium.

In 1998, Tischler won a competition to produce artwork for the swimming and diving facility. In collaboration with friend and painter Ken McDonald of New Mexico, Tischler created a massive 14-foot by 300-foot glazed masterpiece — one of the largest tile murals in North America.

Created from 17,000 bisque tiles, the mural depicts four different seascapes, including an ocean storm, incoming surf, hammerhead sharks, and an abstract underwater scene with fish swimming through rays of sunshine.

"With the piece, I wanted the viewing public to get the visual feel of water shimmering off a large pool and to also get the sensation that the person viewing it was under water," Tischler said. "It's just meant to be a fun, whimsical piece of art."

The process of creating such a huge, technically demanding piece took two years, said Tischler, who equated the project to a "really big adventure." He and McDonald rented a large studio at the Midtown Complex near the Denver Coliseum, located north of downtown Denver. Assembling the piece required expansive warehouse space, where the artists could erect scaffolding and adhere the thousands of six-inch tiles to the walls using two-way tape.

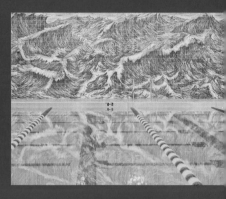

Film transparencies of Tischler's original design schematic were then projected onto the walls, allowing McDonald to trace the design onto the tiles. Afterward, the two artists applied a paint-like substance made of ceramic oxides and colorants to the tiles — a process made time intensive by the substance's rough consistency. Once the tiles were painted, they were fired on site.

Tischler installed the piece himself, but only after the man he hired to do the job predicted that several boxes of tiles would be lost to breakage. Shocked, Tischler fired the artisan and took over the scaffolding — without, he added, breaking even one tile.

---

student lounge of the Rocky Mountains. For students working hard to master their art, the rose window is all theirs, a symbol of appreciation for a job well done.

CELEBRATING THE CREATIVITY OF WOMEN

At the Chambers Center for the Advancement of Women, a number of installations celebrate the creative efforts of women while inspiring ambition in their daughters. A Wiener/Caricof limestone relief in the courtyard garden features six figures tied together by a variety of textures and anchored by a shared horizon line. The figure at the left signifies strength and vision, while the figure depicted in the left foreground can be interpreted as Mother Earth. The two centered figures are celebrating life, while the two figures to the right express education, compassion, friendship, and motherhood.

In addition to the limestone relief, the building features the handiwork of DU alumna Sharon Anhorn, whose metal and glass creations were much admired by Childress. In fact, Childress had commissioned Anhorn to produce a copper and gold frieze for Ritchie's Kremmling ranch, and he also asked her to fabricate the copper relief *Pro Veritate* that adorns the north entrance to University Hall. In addition, one of her stained-glass creations had a place of honor at Meadow's Edge, his home in Castle Rock.

For the Chambers Center, whose tenants wanted art by women, Anhorn first produced an abstract stone-and-copper medallion weighing 400 pounds. Positioned at the building's entranceway, the abstract, art deco-style sculpture was created to complement the curves and elevation of the building itself. Anhorn worked closely with Michele "Mike" Bloom, then dean of the Women's College, and architect Jane Loefgren to fashion a piece that belonged to the building while reflecting the work within. Anhorn also strove to tap into Childress' sensibilities. "Cab and I had worked together enough that I understood how his design was pulled from the old buildings in Europe. I just wanted this piece to have warmth," she said. "My goal was to produce a piece that would be uplifting, reflecting hope; solid, reflecting strength; fluid, reflecting flexibility; and straightforward, reflecting direction and intent."

LAWRENCE ARGENT'S
WHISPERS

Professor Lawrence Argent's *Whispers* is a guaranteed conversation starter.

Located outside the south entrance to the Ritchie Center, the buffed limestone sculpture raises questions and invites speculation. Why are those lips levitating in mid-air? What did those benches just say?

Argent, an internationally renowned artist with a host of public art installations to his credit, welcomes the reactions that greet his piece, which he considers a "vehicle of communication that gets transmitted across campus." As a professor in DU's School of Art and Art History, Argent celebrates the talk that enlivens a university setting.

Whispers features five elevated sets of human lips in bronze. Each set rests atop a towering pillar, and the five pillars form a circle so that the lips appear to be conversing. To keep the conversation going, four limestone benches, also shaped like human lips, are positioned over a below-grade device that plays pre-recorded discussions. The discourse is activated whenever anyone sits on the bench. When all the benches are occupied, the tableau captures the liveliness of the university dialogue.

The sculpture is intended to engage passersby and to reflect the many conversations that occur in an institution dedicated to exchanging ideas and knowledge. Its subtle curves mimic the rolling landscape that surrounds the Ritchie Center.

Like other Argent works — including *I See What You Mean*, the giant blue bear that peers into the Colorado Convention Center in downtown Denver — *Whispers* triggers a double take. Its full personality is revealed only after reflection and repeated encounters.

At roughly the same time that she was completing the medallion, Anhorn also produced a six-foot oval window for a third-floor classroom on the Chambers Center's west side. Like much of the art in the building, *Mothers' Window* acknowledges the relationships that enhance women's lives. Its shimmering glass textures and embedded elements suggest the richness and complexity of the female experience. To express a sense of whimsy, the window features handmade glass "jewels" the size of quarters and silver dollars. Each fused jewel was kiln-fired and then incorporated into the larger glass pane.

Still other windows, these at the Graduate School of Social Work's Rebecca T. and James P. Craig Hall, do double duty, illuminating spaces and providing artistic inspiration. Craig Hall features four separate window designs by Chicago artist Larry Zgoda, who was chosen from a pool of artists in a nationwide competition.

Using cut, ground, and polished Swarovski crystals, Zgoda aimed to produce, in his words, "genuine and permanent beauty in the built environment." Philosophically, Zgoda was on the same page as the architectural team, believing that his glasswork should transcend the decorative to enhance the entire design of the space. He also shared a fascination with the properties of his materials, enjoying crystal, for example, because of the angles and patterns suggested by its linear structure.

In the oval-shaped *Tree of Life* window on the building's top floor, Zgoda incorporated crystallized glass to create dramatic rainbow tones of reflective interior light. Zgoda also designed this piece to act as a "visual veil" between the inside and outside. It was also crafted as a beacon window representing Colorado's landscape. When lit from the inside, the window glows enticingly, inviting pedestrians to come closer for a better view. "My idea was that the window be a less identifiable and literal interpretation of a tree and instead, more an icon or ornamental piece," Zgoda said.

ART GLASS WINDOWS BY CHICAGOAN LARRY ZGODA CREATE A VISUAL VEIL IN CRAIG HALL. ZGODA'S WORK IS KNOWN FOR ITS GEOMETRIC ELEGANCE AND ITS MIXTURE OF TEXTURE, COLOR, AND PATTERN. HIS CRAIG HALL INSTALLATIONS INCORPORATE IMAGES FROM NATURE TO LINK THE INDOOR ROOMS TO THE OUTDOORS.

The elliptical window on the second floor, as well as the window surrounds at the entranceway and in the Commons Room, all have little crystal "jewels" embedded in them. The effect of filtered, natural daylight as it dances around the walls makes the space an ever-changing and inspirational environment.

FURNITURE AS ART

All of the new and renovated buildings on campus feature furniture by DU alumnus Daniel Strawn of Arcadia Design in Boulder, Colorado. His hand-carved tables, chairs, podiums, bookcases, and cabinets in white oak, cherry, and mahogany are found in classrooms and conference rooms, in common areas and offices.

A longtime collaborator with Childress, Strawn's western-inspired designs complement the materials and aesthetic at play in the university's buildings. Functionally honest and timeless, Strawn's creations remind visitors that they have entered a DU building, they are sitting at a DU table and relaxing in a DU chair. These pieces, Strawn said, "knit the campus together and give it a sense of place and presence."

In addition to the everyday tables and chairs in use across campus, Strawn also designed the appellate court bench in the Ricketson Law Building's moot courtroom. Made of cherry and white oak, this three-sectioned bench features a full-length copper frieze portraying Colorado's Front Range, from Pikes Peak in the south to Longs Peak in the north. The frieze was designed and fabricated by Strawn's wife, Karen, a metalsmith and business partner. As Rodgers noted, their handiwork represents the perfect blend of form and function. "It's more than a piece of furniture — it's a piece of art," he said. "There is a dignity and care that is quite literally tactile and is something you want to reach and touch."

For the free-spirited Strawn, the opportunity to work with Childress and Ritchie was a valuable learning experience that helped him grow artistically. Childress and Ritchie provided a generous — even frightening — dose of freedom, all while demanding that Strawn's work meet high standards for craftsmanship and beauty. Typically, Childress declined to give detailed direction, preferring instead to speak of a commission's goals. "Don't tell Daniel what to do, tell him what you need," Strawn said, paraphrasing Childress' directive to on-campus clients.

"When I first met Cab, I was scared to death of the guy," Strawn recalled. Trying to meet Childress' unspecified criteria forced Strawn to take his designs to the very edge. That willingness to experiment with everything from form to materials made him a favorite of Childress', and the two enjoyed a productive relationship for more than two decades.

In his work for DU, which continues to this day, Strawn chooses the wood for custom pieces based on what the architect has in mind for the building in question. Whether working in cherry or mahogany, Strawn designs each piece to be versatile, timeless, and distinctive. Assisted by his apprentice, Jason Hicks, Strawn also works to maximize the different characteristics of each wood — how it moves, breathes, and changes color over time. "I don't recycle ideas. I always want to give something a fresh look," Strawn said.

Not one to use computers to generate designs, Strawn relies on tried-and-true Old World methods to produce furniture meant to withstand the test of time. For example, he joins two pieces of wood using mortise and tenon construction, a practice used by woodworkers for thousands of years.

"The energy I put into each piece of furniture I make gives that chair, table, or bookcase its own presence," Strawn said. "If you do something nice, people respect it."

THE FURNITURE DESIGNS OF DU ALUMNUS DANIEL STRAWN APPEAR IN BUILDINGS ACROSS CAMPUS.
HIS THREE-SECTIONED BENCH IN THE RICKETSON LAW BUILDING'S MOOT COURTROOM INCORPORATES
A FULL-LENGTH COPPER FRIEZE BY HIS WIFE, KAREN, AN ACCOMPLISHED COPPER/SILVER/GOLDSMITH.

The American West is characterized by inspiring landscapes—mountain vistas that speak to sky-high aspirations and sweeping prairies that offer unlimited horizons. A campus with peaks due west and plains due east needs to bridge the contrast by offering tantalizing views and elbow room for exploration. Just as important, it needs to provide a fertile setting for personal growth.

LANDSCAPES TO INSPIRE LEARNING

9

"I am glad to know the American student of tomorrow will not be doomed to cement campuses, but will always have this jewel of greenery, flowing water, and fountains."

— *LADY BIRD JOHNSON*
At the September 10, 1965, dedication of the Harper Humanities Gardens

THE UNIVERSITY'S WINDING RED-BRICK PATHWAYS, ALONG WITH LIGHT POLES AND TRASH RECEPTACLES PAINTED A CRANBERRY RED, CONTRIBUTE TO THE INSTITUTION'S SENSE OF PLACE. THE MEANDERING PATHS COMPLEMENT THE CONTOURS OF THE LANDSCAPE AND SIGNIFY THE COURSE OF A STUDENT'S EDUCATION ODYSSEY.

More than four decades ago, Lady Bird Johnson, then first lady of the United States, came to the University of Denver campus to plant a pin oak tree next to the Evans Chapel. As the nation's foremost champion of beautification and regional landscaping, Mrs. Johnson saw the dedication of the Harper Humanities Gardens as an opportunity to advance her views about the importance of green space. Her presence complemented the goals of Chancellor Chester M Alter, who believed that beautiful settings make for rewarding learning environments.

Alter's efforts at campus landscaping represented one of the university's first cohesive attempts to create a pleasing outdoor environment. When construction first began on University Hall in the 1890s, little thought was given to the spaces around the building, though Rufus "Potato" Clark, in transferring his land to the university, stipulated that the institution beautify the grounds by planting 1,000 trees. As a result, a number of wind-swept specimens dotted the campus landscape.

In succeeding decades, green space was occasionally added but not always tended. All too often, particularly during the post-World War II years, lawns and gardens were sacrificed to make room for Quonset huts and hastily constructed dormitories. By the 1960s, with the country cleaning up highways and byways at the behest of President Lyndon Johnson's Highway Beautification Act, the university leadership was finally ready to think about landscape with some of the same attention devoted to buildings. Unfortunately, many of the proposals to spruce up the campus did not survive budget review. "The first thing that always gets cut on every project is the landscaping," longtime land-use planner John Prosser noted with frustration.

Consequently, a mere twenty years after Lady Bird Johnson's visit, Harper's verdant garden had given way to a tangled thicket. Shrubs and trees were either overgrown or spindly. Lawns were choked with weeds, while dandelions dominated the flowerbeds. Worse, trash and litter were scattered everywhere. It was a campus in decline, a casualty of the university's struggle to survive.

PRUNING, PLANTING, AND IMPROVING

Possessed of a green thumb and a fondness for botanic displays, Dan Ritchie would have made landscape improvement a top priority under any circumstances. But enhancing the campus' outdoor environment was about more than satisfying his urge to beautify. It was a business decision. After all, a campus' grounds provide the raw material for first impressions. And for prospective students and potential donors, initial impressions can make a big difference.

For his first steps, Ritchie drew upon lessons he learned while working as an entertainment executive in Hollywood, where he owned a house originally built for actress Elizabeth Taylor. After remodeling the inside and planting flowers outside, he asked a close friend—a woman known for her exquisite taste—to review his efforts. "It's really good…the furnishings and all; however, you've missed the most important aspect…the trees," Ritchie recalled her saying.

He then hired a qualified arborist to shape the trees, which turned them into, in his words, "a work of art." This single act transformed his home, and Ritchie became a proponent of prudent pruning. "You want to shape the spaces and allow the views," he said.

Pruning made a huge difference at DU as well, but it was only the beginning. Subsequent improvements were made incrementally and in conjunction with emerging plans for new buildings. "Before Dan undertook any major landscaping projects," Mark Rodgers said, "he first wanted to make sure we could take care of something simple like brick walkways, light poles, tree canopies, or strategic flower gardens. In regard to the landscaping, it was much more of a gradual process. It just took longer for people to understand the value of green spaces."

The first major landscaping project was launched in 1997 and centered around Graduation Green, which Rodgers tackled along with landscape designer Charles Rapp, who operated a consulting firm based in California. A longtime associate of Childress', Rapp was charged with creating an attractive space using resilient plantings and requiring modest maintenance. He also needed to accommodate a grove of mature trees. "That, to me, was the biggest challenge," Rapp recalled, noting that every change in grade, every introduction of a pathway or planting had to be accomplished without disturbing the soil around the trees. A second challenge involved unifying the circulation system. To do this, Rapp introduced pathways on a series of

THE UNIVERSITY IS ONE OF SIXTY U.S. COLLEGES TO HOST AN ARBORETUM ON CAMPUS. THE CHESTER M ALTER ARBORETUM, NAMED AFTER A MUCH-RESPECTED FORMER CHANCELLOR WHO CHAMPIONED EFFORTS TO BEAUTIFY THE CAMPUS, SERVES AS A LIVING LABORATORY OF TREES AND SHRUBS. ITS COLLECTION INCLUDES ROUGHLY 400 SPECIES.

oval formations. These routed pedestrians to each building while conforming to the contours of the land.

The Rodgers-Rapp collaboration continued with the remaking of Old Science Green. Again, the two worked with a durable, simple, and minimal palette: existing trees, lawn, a hilly landform, and winding walkways. Today, the green breaks up the buildings that face Evans Avenue and allows passing motorists a view of the interior campus.

THE LURE OF THE BRICK PATH

Ritchie also borrowed from his Hollywood years when making another critical decision about the grounds. One of the most notable improvements he made to his California home was to replace concrete walks with brick paths. This simple step made a huge aesthetic difference, and given the preponderance of brick in DU's new and old buildings, he was sure it would enhance the campus and prove a sound investment. Besides allowing moisture to penetrate tree roots below them, the red brick of the walkways provides a visually appealing symmetry to the surrounding buildings. The bricks also age well and have proved easy to maintain.

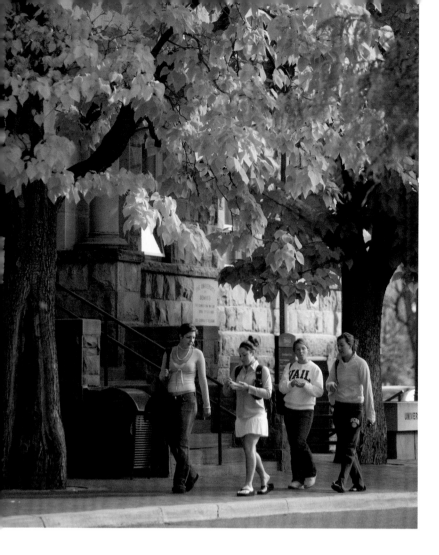

Once funds were allocated, the campus' hard-pan gravel paths were torn up and replaced with elegantly curved walkways. "We tried to put a straight walk in, but Dan said, 'No, it's got to have a bit of a curve,'" Childress said. Not only was the curve deemed pleasing to the eye, it was also a representation of the winding and wandering course of a student's educational odyssey. "The best things about all of these buildings is not the destinations, but the paths along the way," Rodgers said.

The paths also serve to support another university priority: fostering connections across disciplines and divisions. As they wend their way from one building to another, students and faculty meet each other in unexpected places. They round a bend to see a building in a different light. They choose an alternate route to a destination and explore different corners of the campus along the way.

Just as important, Prosser said, the brick paths tell pedestrians they are on the University of Denver campus. "DU's brick walkways are so wonderful because they give you the feeling of being in some place like Charleston, South Carolina. Those walkways literally tie the whole campus together."

GREEN SPACES AND GARDENS FOR STUDENT USE

The concept of green space as an integral component of a university environment has animated campus designers since the nineteenth century. In designing the University of Virginia, for example, Thomas Jefferson sited his celebrated Academical Village around an expansive lawn. Between 1857 and 1950, Frederick Law Olmstead and his sons designed hundreds of college landscapes, including Stanford University in Palo Alto, California, and Smith College in Northampton, Massachusetts. Known as the founder of American landscape architecture, Olmsted believed passionately in the artistic integration of greenscapes and architecture—on campuses, in parks, and in civic settings.

Twenty-first century campus designers see many advantages to greenscaping. First, thoughtfully designed green spaces produce a number of environmental benefits—providing summer shade to boost energy conservation and absorbing rainfall runoff, to name just two. More important, landscape architect Spencer Nickel, hired in 2000 to help DU handle the landscape issues associated with construction of the Ricketston Law Building, maintains that careful

"THE BEST THINGS ABOUT THESE BUILDINGS," SAID UNIVERSITY ARCHITECT MARK RODGERS, "ARE NOT THE DESTINATIONS BUT THE PATHS ALONG THE WAY."

landscape management makes for a better student experience. Not only do green and open spaces serve to facilitate campus circulation, he said, they also "order and organize outdoor gatherings and events and provide some of the most memorable campus spaces when the university experience is later reflected upon."

The importance of the student experience guided much of Nickel's thinking about one of the university's key open spaces, Campus Green. For many years, Campus Green — bordered by Evans Avenue to the south and Asbury Street to the north — was a nondescript lawn used for a variety of campus social events. During construction of the Ricketson Law Building and its parking facilities, Campus Green was temporarily converted to a parking lot.

That gave Nickel the opportunity to reimagine Campus Green and to transform it into a welcoming outdoor retreat. Nickel's plans called for creation of a retaining wall bordered by flowering shrubs, as well as a spacious lawn suitable for impromptu Frisbee matches and picnics. Because the Driscoll Student Center opens to the green, it is the ideal spot for student recreation. With Nickel's vision realized, the green is now used extensively in all four seasons.

The garden just to the east of the Campus Green and right outside the west entrance of the Ricketson Law Building was initially influenced by Ritchie, who, on a trip to Japan, had become intrigued by the country's tradition of garden design. In its first years, that garden featured some 40,000 pansies, planted to offer an aerial view of a yellow-petaled, white-centered flower. Today, the bed has been transformed into an eight-point compass rose, a directional symbol used on maps and nautical charts since the Middle Ages. The flagstone points of the compass rose are true compass directions. The flagstone's hard surface also provides gardeners a footpath to the farthest reaches of the bed, allowing them to add plantings when the pansies wilt or change color.

Another area that needed attention was the Harper Humanities Gardens, located just to the west of the Mary Reed Building. To reveal the gardens' bone structure, the grounds crew removed a significant number of juniper bushes that had encroached around parts of the water features. These overgrown shrubs were replaced by perennial beds, bringing some welcome color to the garden's summer incarnation. In addition, the primary water feature was enlivened with a representation of exotic water lilies and other aquatic specimens.

JUDICIOUS LANDSCAPING HAS CREATED AN ENVIRONMENT THAT ENCOURAGES BOTH COMMUNITY AND QUIET REFLECTION. LANDSCAPING EFFORTS HAVE ALSO PRESERVED AND ENHANCED MOUNTAIN VIEWS.

Carnegie Green, which runs from the Daniels College of Business to the east down to the School of Hotel, Restaurant, and Tourism Management to the west, was improved by the addition of spectacular perennial gardens that offer interest from early spring to mid fall. The garden is framed by a granite wall and punctuated by a handful of benches that offer students peaceful areas for study. The walls on the green were meant to "imply a visual 'base' to the surrounding buildings as viewed from the green, and to enclose the landform of the ceremonial garden space adjacent to Mary Reed," Nickel said. The nearby Buchtel Tower shelters a grove of flowering trees that complement the structure's coloring and stature. The trees were planted in recognition of the tower's rich history and the integral role it plays as a campus landmark.

Nickel urged DU officials to focus on balancing how buildings and green space work together to make the campus more inviting. "The campus framework is not entirely informed by the surrounding urban grid," he said. Instead, it departs radically from the streets and cross streets that serve a big-city car culture, funneling drivers onto major arteries.

Although DU is bordered, and even bisected, by traffic-heavy avenues and boulevards, it is not a driver's campus. Rather, an internal greensward, designed and preserved by previous generations, flows through campus like a river, taking pedestrians, bikers, and skateboarders—not drivers—to various academic, social, and administrative destinations.

Today, the university's mix of greenscapes provides a lush setting for outdoor life. It is not uncommon to find a professor leading a class discussion under an oak tree, coeds lunching in the Harper Humanities Gardens, or a group of students sunning themselves on the grassy expanse of Campus Green.

That delights Rodgers, who believes the university has learned much about how to create a unified landscape that complements the institution's mission. With each project, the design team has learned lessons and re-evaluated its approach to green spaces. "We first built buildings, then added landscape, then designed buildings with landscape, and then designed landscape without buildings," said Rodgers. "Now we have reached the point where landscape and architecture are melded, and neither is secondary to the other."

MASTERMINDING A LAND USE PLAN

Aesthetic and landscape improvements to the University Park campus were only part of the transformation agenda. By 1999, Ritchie, Childress, and Rodgers also recognized that if the campus' 128 acres were to be used wisely and efficiently, the institution needed a land use plan.

In the spring of 2000, DU hired Massachusetts-based Shepley Bulfinch Richardson & Abbott to work with Rodgers in developing a land use plan that would provide a stable vision for the campus, one that would offer guidelines for growth and development. In 2002, the plan was completed. It was updated in 2007, in part to reflect the university's formal commitment to sustainability principles. Both the original plan and the update were authored with a two-decade shelf life in mind.

Besides highlighting DU's goals of building efficiently, the plan addressed ecological issues, particularly water conservation and pesticide reduction. It defined the campus' perimeters and provided guidelines for pedestrian and bicycle circulation. Just as important, the plan explored the creation of a central promenade linking the far corners and all the greens of the campus. Although still a work in progress, the promenade has done much to accentuate the pedestrian nature of the campus, connecting the science end of campus with the athletics end, linking the arts programs with the residential buildings. By doing so, it fosters a sense of identity and community among those who learn, teach, and work at the university.

"The plan has brought a broader consensus of understanding about how the university will grow," Rodgers explained. "We work with it as a way to guide the often unpredictable events that lead to new projects."

THE CHESTER M ALTER ARBORETUM

On Friday, April 30, 1999, more than 150 past and present faculty members, alumni, trustees, and friends of the university gathered for the dedication ceremony of the Chester M Alter Arboretum on the University Park campus. With that ceremony, the Alter Arboretum joined the Denver Botanic Gardens as one of only two arboreta in the state.

It was an especially poignant moment for former DU Chancellor Chester M Alter, then 93 years old. The ceremony capped a four-decade effort to recognize the plethora of

THE UNIVERSITY LANDSCAPE HAS EVOLVED GRADUALLY
AND IN ACCORDANCE WITH THE INSTITUTION'S MISSION.
AS CHESTER ALTER, WHO SERVED AS UNIVERSITY
CHANCELLOR FROM 1953 TO 1966, ONCE SAID, "A LOT
OF LEARNING TAKES PLACE IN THE OPEN SPACES
BETWEEN BUILDINGS."

exquisite trees on campus. An environmentalist from a very early age, Alter brought his enthusiasm and love of trees and plants to DU. During his tenure as chancellor from 1953 to 1967, he was influential in beautifying the campus. His passion ran so deep that he likened trees to people. "If a tree is to be our friend," he once said, "then we should be able to call it by name, just as we do when we pass a human being."

To qualify as an arboretum, the campus needed to offer visitors an educational experience, one in which they could identify labeled trees, shrubs, and woody plants. After a geography student mapped each of the campus' 1,865 trees utilizing an aerial photograph, David Christophel, then director of the arboretum, and arborist Marc Hathaway proceeded to identify each of the 400 or more species on campus.

The arboretum director's job includes keeping an accurate inventory of the trees, expanding the campus' collection of trees in a specified manner, strategically positioning new species, and developing an aesthetically pleasing environment. The university's facilities management team, meanwhile, ensures that trees and shrubs are properly pruned and maintained.

Prior to his departure from the university in late 2007, Christophel introduced a number of non-native species, including maples, chestnuts, and even two redwoods, located in a grove north of Cherrington Hall and west of the Mary Reed Building. A trained paleontologist, Christophel wanted to include the redwoods in the collection as "living fossils" of the many species that populated Colorado long, long ago. Despite drought and Colorado's ever-changing and extreme weather, two conditions generally regarded as unfriendly to redwoods, the two trees are holding their own.

Throughout the seasons, the arboretum serves as what Alter called a "living laboratory" in which students— particularly those interested in biology, geology, and ecology —come face to face with everything from the eastern white pine and horse chestnut to the western catalpa and yellow buckeye. But the arboretum also serves as a community resource, a place where Denver citizens can learn about the trees that grace the city.

"We are a living community, not just a bunch of buildings," said Bob Dores, chair of the Department of Biology, whose faculty members consider the arboretum an educational resource. "We take in the ecology of the entire environment and try to make it a better place for everyone."

WATER WONDERS

The meandering water feature in the Harper Humanities Gardens just west of the Mary Reed Building comes to life each spring and summer with a display of beautiful tropical plants.

The recirculating warm waters nourish a plethora of water lilies. Specimens native to the United States and Europe offer a fireworks display of white, pink, red, and yellow blossoms. A tropical assortment of lilies native to South America and Africa pull from the blue and purple end of the color spectrum. Among the exhibit's showpieces are the Victoria water lily indigenous to Brazil, whose leaves can grow to seven feet in diameter, and the lively white, pink, and red lotus flowers, some known as "changeables" because they change color from day to day.

The exhibit is enhanced by flora known as marginals—aquatic vegetation with nonflowering leaves. These include the water iris, cattails, taro, and cyperus.

DU's horticulture staff preserves these plants during the cold months by carefully removing each one after the fall's first frost, usually in October. The plants are nourished during the winter months and reintroduced into their water environs each spring.

For assistance with the collection, the university maintains a collaborative relationship with the horticulture staff at the Denver Botanic Gardens. Joe Tomocik, curator of the Denver Botanic Gardens' own water features, considers the DU display an ambitious undertaking for a university.

"I can't imagine a university campus with as many different types of flowers as those at DU," Tomocik says. "By combining these various types of plants, you get to design and arrange them as you want and create your own story."

INDEX

ACKNOWLEDGMENTS

University Communications would like to thank the following individuals and organizations for their many contributions to the preparation of this book:

- Chancellor Emeritus Daniel Ritchie

- Chancellor Robert Coombe

- Provost Gregg Kvistad

- Craig Woody, vice chancellor of Business and Financial Affairs

- Joy Burns, Pat Livingston, Donald Sturm, University of Denver Board of Trustees

- Carl Williams, honorary life trustee

- Penny Childress Alexander, Jim Childress, John Childress, Lee Childress

- The staff at the Western History and Genealogy Department, Denver Public Library

- Joe Tomocik, Denver Botanic Gardens

- Steve Fisher, Marcia Kehl, Claire Williamson, Archives and Special Collections, University of Denver

- Bill Campbell, Vicky Garfias-O'Brien, Jane Loefgren, Mark Rodgers, Office of the University Architect

- Claire Brownell, Kristi Burgert, Teri Coe, Office of the Chancellor

- Carol Farnsworth, Jim Berscheidt, Grace Stanton, Amyanne Rasberry Matthias, Christa Bruning, University Communications

- The many members of the University of Denver community who shared their experiences and memories

- The artists, artisans, landscape architects, and architects whose stories grace this book

- The countless donors whose generosity brought these buildings to life

Photography

Many of the photographs in this book come from University of Denver collections. Others are courtesy of the following individuals and entities:

- Wayne Armstrong, University Communications; Tim Ryan, formerly of University Communications

- Michael Richmond Photography

- Matt Slater Photography (photographs of the Chambers Center, pages 100, 105, 107–109)

- Andrews & Anderson Architects PC and Windsong Imagery (photographs of Craig Hall and Fisher Early Learning Center, pages 131, 133, 135, 169, and 172)

- *The Denver Post* (photographs of Cab Childress on pages 31, 41–43; of Dan Ritchie and Childress on pages 34 and 36; of Childress, Ritchie and Mark Rodgers on page 99)

- 9NEWS, Amelia Earhart (aerial photograph, page 39)

- Daniel Strawn (photographs on page 191)

- Daniels College of Business, Vicki Kerr Photography (photographs on pages 60, 61, 63, 65)

Built for Learning. A Unified Architectural Vision for the University of Denver

Published by:

University of Denver

2199 S. University Blvd.

Denver, CO 80208

www.du.edu

ISBN: 978-0-9648871-3-8

Library of Congress Control Number: 2008906616

Executive Editor:

Carol Farnsworth, University Communications

Managing Editor:

Tamara Chapman, University Communications

Creative Director:

Jim Good, University Communications

Research and Copy:

George Brown, Timelines Commemorative Histories

Tamara Chapman, University Communications

Art Direction and Design:

Mark Mulvany, Mark Mulvany Graphic Design

Design and Production:

Tim George, I Design of Denver, Inc.

Printer:

Friesens of Altona, Manitoba

Manufactured in Canada

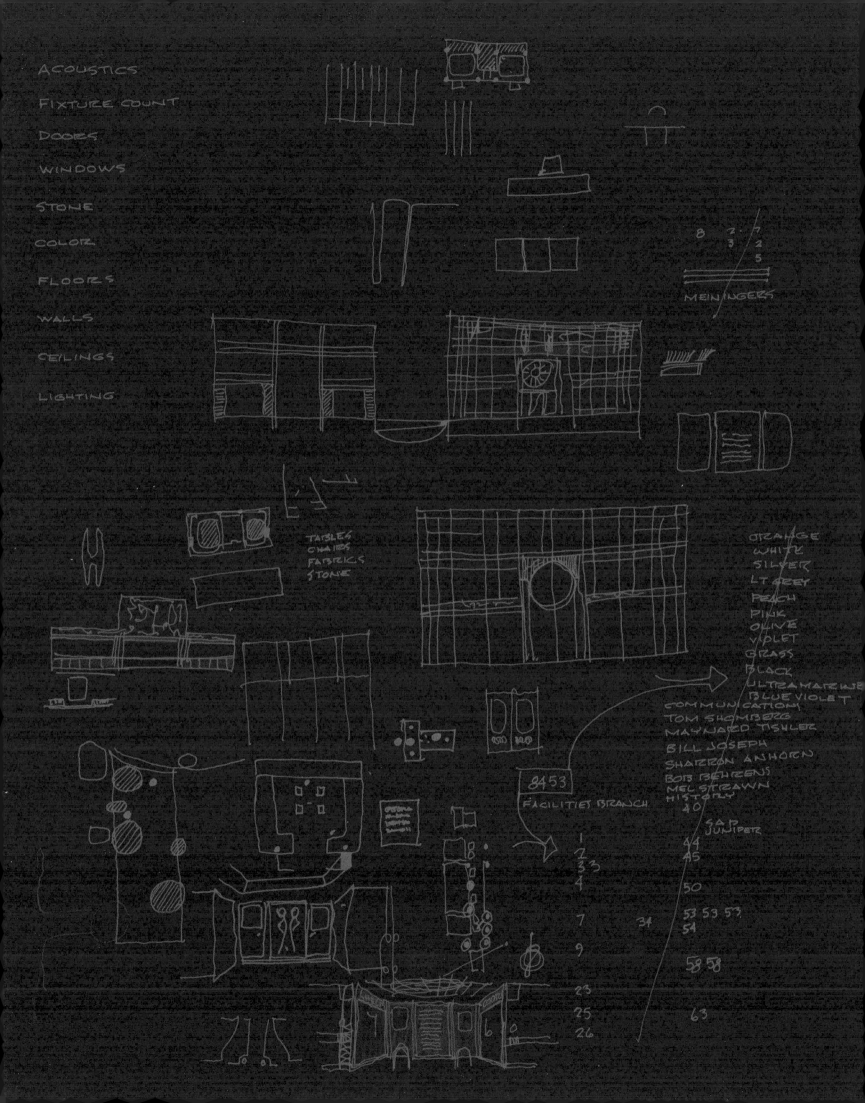

ACOUSTICS

FIXTURE COUNT

DOORS

WINDOWS

STONE

COLOR

FLOORS

WALLS

CEILINGS

LIGHTING

MEININGERS

TABLES
CHAIRS
FABRICS
STONE

ORANGE
WHITE
SILVER
LT GREY
PEACH
PINK
OLIVE
VIOLET
GRASS
BLACK
ULTRAMARINE
BLUE VIOLET
COMMUNICATIONS
TOM SHOMBERG
MAYNARD TISHLER
BILL JOSEPH
SHARRON ANHORN
BOB BEHRENS
MEL STRAWN
HISTORY
40

SAP
JUNIPER

8453
FACILITIES BRANCH